THE CHILDREN'S HOUR

BY
LILLIAN HELLMAN

★

★

DRAMATISTS
PLAY SERVICE
INC.

2

THE BIGGER THE LIE

This article is reprinted from the *New York Times* of December 14, 1952, by the kind permission of the *Times* and of the author, Harry Gilroy.

The play which turned a nice quiet young woman named Lillian Hellman into one of the best-known modern playwrights— *The Children's Hour*—again comes to life in all its tragic fascination Thursday night at the Coronet. Most people interested in the theater probably know this is a drama about a girl in a boarding school who spreads the story that two women have an abnormal attachment for one another. Theatergoers may know also that it was a great success— it ran 691 performances starting in November, 1934—but few can realize the controversies it created behind the scenes.

Miss Hellman recounted these doings a few days ago in a whisper. The sotto voce effect was not to keep eavesdroppers from hearing, since she was alone with the interviewer in the spacious, fire-brightened drawing room of her Manhattan apartment. It was simply that she had weakened her voice when she began to direct the company which will present the play and, after several weeks of rehearsals conducted by microphone, her vocal cords had gone on strike.

Among the things she confided in her whisper was that it had been impossible to get any of Broadway's leading ladies to take roles in the original production. Alice Brady and other actresses were afraid police would close the play. But it scored a critical success and then, Miss Hellman recalled, there was talk that it had a chance for the Pulitzer Prize. "However, the rumor was that Professor William Lyon Phelps of Yale refused to attend the play," Miss Hellman said, "and he was the Pulitzer play committee in those days." (The award went to a drama by Zoë Akins, called *The Old Maid*, based on a story by Edith Wharton.)

Apart from the excitement stirred by *The Children's Hour*, it was a remarkable performance for a young writer. "I'd had a couple of little stories published," Miss Hellman said. "I was married to Arthur Kober at that time and these stories appeared in a magazine of which he was an editor. Not, of course, that that was the reason for their publication. And I'd written, with Louis Kronenberger, a comedy about a royal family who wanted to be middle-class people—that play was always being bought but never produced. Then I read the book which gave rise to *The Children's Hour*."

The book was William Roughead's *Bad Companions*, which was published in Scotland in 1930. In one chapter entitled "Closed Doors, or The Great Drumsheugh Case," there is the story of a scandal in Edinburgh in 1809, caused by a malicious child who said that the two headmistresses at her school had "an inordinate affection" for each other.

Lillian Hellman, 26 years old, a writer of no considerable experience, took this theme and made it into a play which has been widely praised for dramatic intensity and psychological insight. Reflecting on how she had achieved such a result, Miss Hellman said: "One thing that has struck me about *The Children's Hour* is that anyone young ordinarily writes autobiographically. Yet I picked on a story that I could treat with complete impersonality. I hadn't even been to boarding school—I went to school here in New York.

"Here's another observation I make about the play today as I work over it. On the stage a person is twice as villainous as, say, in a novel. When I read that story I thought of the child as neurotic, sly, but not the utterly malignant creature which playgoers see in her. I never see the characters as monstrously as the audiences do—in her case I saw her as a bad character but never outside life. It's the results of her lie that make her so dreadful—this is really not a play about lesbianism, but about a lie. The bigger the lie the better, as always."

The author had a maid bring in coffee to sluice over the rasping vocal cords. "That's a little better," she said. "Perhaps I got this affliction because I was uneasy about working on the play before I began. Kermit Bloomgarden, the producer, wanted it revived. Of course I did, too—no one likes money more than I do—and beyond that you don't like to see a work die. A writer must want money and want people to like what he writes—but the important thing is wanting but not writing for it, if you know what I mean. Anyhow, when I got into the work, I felt this was a good play to be doing again because it isn't about a time or a movement. It's a story."

What work has Miss Hellman done on her play? "Oh, some lines seemed slightly literary, and I've changed them. Then I had a great temptation to rewrite it. In a sense I had to stand by the play. What you did some years ago, you did that day. Eighteen years later you are a different person with a whole different series of emotions. I was afraid that I'd be weepy, but I wasn't sorry about the lapse of time—I found I'm glad it's past."

The playwright smiled as a kind of philosophical comment on her words. "Well, now we have a fine cast playing *The Children's Hour*. I believe that people who have seen the play before will find that this is in many ways a different interpretation."

Miss Hellman phrased the next query for herself, "But what am I going to tackle after the play opens?" She tried to dredge up the answer under the hypnotic influence of the crackling fire. "You may know that I've been editing the Chekhov letters for that 'Great Letters' series that Louis Kronenberger is bringing out as the overall editor. Now that job is finished, too, so I'm really free to write a play. I do have two or three characters rattling around."

Then she volunteered—"Have I mentioned to you that I thought of doing more about the people of *The Little Foxes*? I've always thought about that story as requiring a trilogy to finish it." She would not say where, in the matter of time, she visualized the third play fitting into the series with *Another Part of the Forest* and *The Little Foxes*.

"All I can say is that I'm a little baffled about the characters I now have in my mind because in the past the characters which rattle around there—as I say—have always been the ones for the play beyond the one I was writing. But at the present I'm not writing one. I don't know whether that's a bad sign or not. In any case, I must get to work. Work engenders work. And at my age I believe it is time that I began to get in a hurry." Miss Hellman gulped another cup of coffee. "It's a miracle," she whispered, "that my voice lasted through this talk."

HARRY GILROY

CAST
(In the order of which they speak)

Peggy Rogers
Catherine
Lois Fisher
Mrs. Lily Mortar
Evelyn Munn
Helen Burton
Rosalie Wells
Janet
Leslie
Mary Tilford
Karen Wright
Martha Dobie
Doctor Joseph Cardin
Agatha
Mrs. Amelia Tilford
A Grocery Boy

Act I
Living room of the Wright-Dobie School.
Late afternoon in April.

Act II
Scene 1: Living room at Mrs. Tilford's.
A few hours later.
Scene 2: The same. Later that evening.

Act III
The same as Act I. November.

THE CHILDREN'S HOUR

ACT I

SCENE: *A room in the Wright-Dobie School for girls, a converted farmhouse eighteen miles from the town of Lancet. It is a comfortable, unpretentious room used as an afternoon study room and at all other times as the living room.*

Downstage R. is a large window through which we see a stone wall covered with ivy. Upstage of the window is a large wooden pilaster supporting the ceiling beam, which runs the length of the room. On the pilaster are two small carriage prints. Upstage of the pilaster, a built-in bookcase filled with books. The bottom shelf is also used to keep pads, pencils, ink, stationery, etc. Stage R. in upstage wall, another bookcase filled with books and bric-a-brac. Center stage, a large door leading to a hallway which leads R. to outside door and L. to other rooms of the house. In the hall is a staircase going off L. There is a chair R. of the stairs against wall. L. of the door, in the upstage wall of the room, is another built-in bookcase similarly filled. On the lower shelf of this bookcase is a telephone. On wall to L. of bookcase is a bulletin board, below it a cabinet, on which are four books and a clock. There is a wastebasket R. of cabinet. Down R. in front of window, is a small oblong table with a table lamp and ashtray. Down R. of table, a Hitchcock chair. Up L. of table, a green upholstered chair. R. C. a large sofa with small round pillows at either end. Beside L. end of sofa a small pie-crust table on which is a large ashtray and a small china kitten, L. C. an oblong desk with a drawer that faces upstage. On desk: inkstand with pen, a bottle of ink, ashtray, pads, pencils, etc. In drawer of desk: examination papers, pads, pencils, cigarettes, matches. R. of desk, a Hitchcock chair. Upstage of desk, a wooden arm-chair with upholstered seat. L. of desk, an upholstered chair with low arms. Down L., below pilaster, is a round checker-board table and Windsor chair. On table, a green-shade student lamp. Down L. a large ornate Franklin stove, beside which, downstage, is an iron coal-or-wood scuttle. Two converted oil lamps hang from ceiling beam, R. and L. of C.

It is early in an afternoon in April.

AT RISE: *Mrs. Lily Mortar is sitting in chair L. of desk, her head back and her eyes closed, holding a book in her lap. She is a florid woman of forty-five with obviously touched-up hair. Her clothes are too fancy for a classroom.*

Eight girls, from twelve to fourteen years old, are informally grouped on chairs and sofa. Janet is seated in chair D. R. of D. R. table. She is sewing on an apron. Helen is seated in chair U. L. of D. R. table, sewing flowers on a red band which is intended for a hat. They both have sewing baskets beside them. Evelyn, kneeling on a pillow beside end of sofa, is using her scissors to trim the hair of Rosalie, who is sitting on floor in front of her. Rosalie is holding a hand mirror, in which she, nervously, follows the trimming of her hair. Lois, frantically studying for a Latin exam, is seated on R. end of sofa. Catherine is seated beside her, reading. Leslie, who is writing in a notebook, is sitting on floor leaning against L. end of sofa. She is facing L. All the girls have school books, notebooks, pencils, candy, etc. beside them.

The eighth girl, Peggy Rogers, is sitting on L. arm of sofa. She is reading aloud from a book. She is bored and reads in a sing-song, tired voice.

PEGGY. *(Reading as curtain rises.)* I hear him mock the luck of Caesar, which the Gods give men to excuse their after wrath: *(Curtain is up, as:)* "Husband, I come. Now to that name my courage prove my title. I am fire, and air; my other elements I give to baser life. So, have you done? Come then, and take the last

8

warmth of my lips. Farewell, kind Charmian; Iras, long farewell." *(Peggy pokes Catherine.)* I kiss you here. *(Rosalie passes some candy to Lois.)*

CATHERINE. Skip it.

PEGGY. Iras? Lois, where are you? You die here.

LOIS. *(Monotonously.)* Ferebam, ferebas, ferebat— *(Looks up from Latin book.)* All right. I'm dead. I'd like to die till after the exam was over and then go swimming. Ferebamus, ferebatis, fere, fere— *(Helen puts red band, on which she has been sewing a flower, on Rosalie's head.)*

CATHERINE. *(To Lois.)* Ferebant.

MRS. MORTAR. *(Opens her eyes.)* Evelyn, what are you doing?

EVELYN. Uh, nothing, Mrs. Mortar.

MRS. MORTAR. You're certainly doing something. It's very unfortunate that you girls cannot sit quietly with your sewing and drink in the immortal words of the immortal bard. There will never be another. *(Evelyn has taken the band from Rosalie's head and puts it on her own.)* What's that thing? Who is sewing on that?

EVELYN. It's a hat for church. You said I couldn't wear that handkerchief again.

MRS. MORTAR. You can't wear *that* to church. Not when I chaperone the school.

HELEN. *(Takes band from Evelyn, puts it on D. R. table.)* Might as well throw it away.

MRS. MORTAR. Throw it away. If ever you had known the pangs of adversity, as I have known them— *(Vaguely.)* Do something else with it. Women must learn these tricks. *(To Peggy and Catherine.)* Continue, please.

PEGGY. Er. "The stroke of death is as a lover's pinch, which hurts, and is desir'd." *(U. C. door has slowly opened and Mary starts to sneak into the room. Catherine sees her, motions her away. Mary slowly and silently exits, closing door.)*

LOIS. *(Unexpectedly, dreamy.)* I know. *(Then she goes back to mumbling the Latin, embarrassed.)*

PEGGY. "Dost thou lie still? If thus thou vanishest, thou tell'st the world it is not worth leave taking." *(Rosalie passes candy to Helen.)*

CATHERINE. "Dissolve thick cloud, and rain; that I may say the Gods themselves do weep."

PEGGY.	LOIS. *(To Catherine.)*	
"This proves me base: If she first	Will you help me with this after class is over?	CATHERINE. I helped you

meet the curled
Antony…"

with it last week.
What's the matter
with you?

MRS. MORTAR. *(Rapping on table.)* We cannot have this. How many people in this room are talking—?

HELEN. Mrs. Mortar, we have exams tomorrow. We have to—

MRS. MORTAR. *(Rises.)* I cannot allow you to use the sewing and elocution hour to learn what you should have been learning the entire past term.

PEGGY. *(Trying to save things, turns to Mrs. Mortar.)* Excuse me. *(Quickly reads again.)* "He'll make demand of her, and spend that kiss which is my Heaven to have. Come, thou mortal wretch—"

MRS. MORTAR. *(Crosses to L. end of sofa. To Peggy.)* You're talking to an asp. You're going to die. Try to feel, try. Try again. I'll give you the cue.

ROSALIE. What's a cue?

MRS. MORTAR. A cue is a line given the actor or actress to remind them of their next speech.

CATHERINE. To remind *him* or *her.*

MRS. MORTAR. *(Motions Catherine to be quiet. Speaks to Peggy, tapping her on the chest.)* "With thy sharp teeth this knot intrinsicate."

CATHERINE. Did he not mean intrinsic?

MRS. MORTAR. *(Glowers at her.)* Be still. "Of life at once untie; poor venomous fool, be angry and dispatch. Peace, peace, dost thou not see my baby at my breast—"

CATHERINE. *(Happily.)* Mrs. Mortar, you skipped two lines. Because I would have said, "O eastern star," but I couldn't say it because you—

MRS. MORTAR. *(Crosses back to chair L. of desk. Sits.)* I never missed a line in my life. Never.

CATHERINE. *(Rises. Crosses toward Mrs. Mortar to show her the book.)* Yes, ma'am. Look. *(Mrs. Mortar holds up her hand to stop Catherine.)*

LOIS. Utor, fruor, fungor, potior and vascor take the dative.

CATHERINE. *(Returns to her place on sofa. Kicks Lois. Sits.)* Take the ablative, stupid.

PEGGY. *(To Catherine.)* You're always correcting somebody.

LOIS. Utor, fruor, fungor, potiar and—

MRS. MORTAR. *(Raps out table.)* Lois, I cannot allow you to interrupt us this way.

LOIS. I'm sorry.

ROSALIE. Were you ever in the movies, Mrs. Mortar?

MRS. MORTAR. I had my offers. It's a shallow art. Not for me. *(Goes back to her book.)*

ROSALIE. *(Evelyn has suddenly snipped another piece. Rosalie looks in mirror.)* Stop it. That's enough. Oh, look what you've done! *(Turns to Evelyn.)* You know what I just think. I think you did it on purpose. That's what I just think. *(Turns downstage.)* But it won't work. I've got my strapless dress. So there.

EVELYN. That I want to see. You in a strapless dress! *(Girls start to giggle.)*

ROSALIE. I say you did it on purpose. Because he's coming to my house.

EVELYN. He's coming to your house because he's your cousin, that's what. A strapless dress— *(All laugh.)*

MRS. MORTAR. *(Becomes aware of noise and raps on table again.)* I want this noise to cease. And I want that silly talk to stop. It is natural that young women should think of young men. But it is not natural until it is proper.

ROSALIE. Mrs. Mortar, was Mr. Mortar very handsome?

MRS. MORTAR. He was an executive. *(Mary Tilford comes in L. door clutching a slightly faded bunch of wildflowers. Door opens far enough to let her squeeze cautiously in. She is fourteen, neither pretty nor ugly. She is an undistinguished-looking girl, except for the sullenly dissatisfied expression on her face. She leaves door open and crosses above D. L. table to L. of Mrs. Mortar.)* Well, young lady, where have you been? You were supposed to read Antony. Where have you been?

MARY. *(Smiling.)* I took a walk.

MRS. MORTAR. Without asking my permission. The result is that I had to read Antony, and I have enough to do. You've been most discourteous. *(To class.)* And courtesy is breeding and breeding is most to be desired in woman. It's what every man wants in woman.

ROSALIE. May I have permission to write that down, Mrs. Mortar?

EVELYN. We wrote it down last week.

MRS. MORTAR. *(To Mary.)* Mary, I am waiting for your explanation. Or I shall most certainly report—

MARY. *(Quickly.)* I am sorry, Mrs. Mortar. I went to get you these flowers. I thought you would like them and I didn't know it would take so long to pick them.

MRS. MORTAR. *(Flattered.)* Well, well.

MARY. You were telling us last week how much you liked flowers, and I thought that I would bring you some and—

MRS. MORTAR. That was very sweet of you, Mary. *(To class.)* I always like thoughtfulness. But you must not allow anything to interfere with your classes. *(To Mary.)* Now run along, dear, and get a vase and some water to put my flowers in. *(Mary turns, sticks out her tongue at class, exits L. Class starts to laugh. Mrs. Mortar looks up, sharply.)*

PEGGY. *(Quickly reads.)* "Oh, Antony. Nay, I will take thee too. What, should *I* stay?"

MRS. MORTAR. You may put that book away, Peggy. I am sure your family need never worry about your going on the stage.

PEGGY. I don't want to go on the stage. I want to be a veterinarian.

MRS. MORTAR. Well, I certainly hope you won't read to the animals. *(Laughter of class pleases her. Girls are making a great show of doing nothing. Rosalie passes candy to Evelyn. Mrs. Mortar puts her head back, closes her eyes.)*

CATHERINE. "How much longer, O Catiline, are you going to abuse our patience?" *(To Lois.)* Now translate it, and for goodness' sakes try to get it right this time. *(She and Lois are murmuring when Karen Wright enters through U. C. door. She leaves door open. Karen is an attractive woman of twenty-eight, casually pleasant in manner, without sacrifice of warmth or dignity. She smiles at girls, goes to above desk. With her entrance there is an immediate change in the manner of the girls: They are fond of her and they respect her. She gives Mrs. Mortar, whose quotation has reached her, an annoyed look. She is carrying some notebooks and papers, which she places on desk.)*

MRS. MORTAR. *(For no reason.)* "As sweet as balm, as soft as air, O Antony—"

JANET. Good afternoon, Miss Wright.

LOIS. "Quo usque tandem a*bu*tere…"

KAREN. *(Automatically.)* Abutere. *(Opens drawer in desk.)*

ROSALIE. *(Rises. Crosses to R. of Karen.)* Look at my hair, Miss Wright. Look at it. Look what Evelyn did—

KAREN. *(Smiling.)* She didn't do good.

EVELYN. *(Giggling.)* I didn't mean to do it that bad, Miss Wright, but Rosalie's got funny hair. I saw a picture in the paper, and I was trying to do it that way.

ROSALIE. *(Feels her hair, looks pathetically at Karen.)* Oh, what shall I do, Miss Wright? *(Gesturing.)* It's long here, and it's short here and—

KAREN. Come up to my room later and I'll see if I can fix it for you. *(Rosalie crosses D.S. to R. of sofa, grabs pillow from under Evelyn, places it on floor in front of R. end of sofa, sits on it.)*

MRS. MORTAR. And hereafter we'll have no more haircutting.

KAREN. Helen, did you look for your bracelet?

HELEN. I've looked everywhere. I can't find it.

KAREN. Have a good look. It must be in your room somewhere. *(Mary comes in from L., with her flowers in a vase. When she sees Karen she loses some of her assurance. Karen looks at flowers in surprise.)*

MARY. *(Crosses R. below desk to D. R. table, places vase on table.)* Good afternoon, Miss Wright. *(Looks at Karen, who is staring hard at flowers.)*

KAREN. Hello, Mary.

MRS. MORTAR. *(Fluttering.)* Peggy has been reading *Cleopatra* for us. *(Peggy sighs.)*

KAREN. *(Smiling.)* Peggy doesn't like *Cleopatra*.

MRS. MORTAR. I don't think she quite appreciates it, but—

KAREN. Well, I didn't, either. *(To Mary, who has moved up to R. of sofa.)* Where'd you get those flowers, Mary?

MRS. MORTAR. She picked them for me. *(Hurriedly.)* It made her a little late to class, but she heard me say I loved flowers, and she went to get them for me. *(With a sigh.)* The first wildflowers of the season.

KAREN. But not the very first, are they, Mary? *(All the girls are watching.)*

MARY. I don't know.

KAREN. Where did you get them?

MARY. Near Conway's cornfield, I think.

KAREN. It wasn't necessary to go so far. There was a bunch exactly like this in the garbage can this morning.

ROSALIE. Oh! *(Girls giggle.)*

MRS. MORTAR. *(After a second, rises.)* Oh, I can't believe it! What a nasty thing to do! Garbage can flowers! *(Crosses R. above sofa to above R. end of sofa. To Mary.)* And I suppose you have just as fine an excuse for being an hour late to breakfast this morning, and last week— *(To Karen.)* I haven't wanted to tell you these things before, but—

KAREN. *(Hurriedly, as school bell rings offstage.)* There's the bell. *(All girls rise, gathering up their books, sewing baskets, etc., and exit through U. C. door. Janet, Helen, and Evelyn cross up behind sofa.*

13

Rosalie, Peggy, Leslie, and Lois cross U. L. of sofa. Mary, attempting a quick and unobtrusive exit, pushes Catherine in front of her, toward L. door. Rosalie, Peggy, and Evelyn go up the stairs. Other girls go L. down hall.)

LOIS. *(The last one, walking toward U. C. door.)* Ad, ab, ante, in, de, inter, con, post, prae—

KAREN. Wait a minute, Mary.

LOIS. *(Looks up at Karen.)* I can't seem to remember the rest. *(Reluctantly Mary stops below chair L. of desk. Catherine crosses above D. L. table, exits L.)*

KAREN. Prae, pro, sub, super. Don't worry, Lois. You'll come out all right. *(Lois smiles, exits through C. door, goes off L., calling to Catherine. Karen picks up two books from floor in front of D. R. end of sofa, puts them on D. R. table, takes pillow from floor R. of sofa, puts it on sofa, takes vase of flowers from D. R. table to desk as she talks.)* Mary, I've had the feeling—and I don't think I'm wrong—that the girls here were happy; that they liked Miss Dobie and me, that they liked the school.

MARY. Miss Wright, I have to get my Latin book. *(Mrs. Mortar comes D. R. of sofa, sits R. end of sofa.)*

KAREN. I thought it was true until you came here a year ago. But I don't think you've been happy here. I've wanted to talk with you many times before but I was hoping that you'd come to me. *(Looks at Mary, waits for an answer, gets none, shakes her head.)* What is the matter, Mary?

MARY. Nothing, Miss Wright.

KAREN. *(In front of desk.)* There must be something wrong or you wouldn't make up these stories so often. Why, for example, do you find it necessary to lie to us so much?

MARY. I'm not lying. I went out walking and I saw the flowers and they looked pretty and I didn't know it was so late.

KAREN. *(Impatiently.)* Stop it, Mary! I'm not interested in hearing that foolish story again. I *know* you got the flowers out of the garbage can. What I do want to know is why you feel you have to lie out of it.

MARY. *(Beginning to whimper.)* I *did* pick the flowers near Conway's. You never believe me. You believe everybody but me. It's always like that. Everything I say you fuss at me about. Everything I do is wrong.

KAREN. You know that isn't true. *(She sits in chair L. of desk and holds Mary's hand.)* Mary, let's try to understand each other. If you

14

feel that you *have* to take a walk, or that you just *can't* come to class, or that you'd like to go to the village by yourself, come and tell me—I'll try and understand. *(Mary slowly removes her hands from Karen's.)* I don't say that I'll always agree that you should do exactly what you want to do. But I've had feelings like that, too—everybody has—and I won't be unreasonable about yours. But this way, this kind of lying you do, makes everything wrong.

MARY. *(Looking steadily at Karen.)* I got the flowers near Conway's cornfield.

KAREN. *(Looks at Mary, sighs, rises, moves U.S. around R. end of desk, stands behind desk for a moment.)* Well, there doesn't seem to be any other way with you; you'll have to be punished. Take your recreation periods alone for the next two weeks. No horseback riding and no hockey. Don't leave the school grounds for any reason whatsoever. Is that clear?

MARY. *(Carefully.)* Saturday, too?

KAREN. Yes.

MARY. But you said I could go to the boat-races.

KAREN. I'm sorry, but you can't go.

MARY. I'll tell my grandmother. I'll tell her how everybody treats me here and the way I get punished for every little thing I do. I'll tell her, I'll—

MRS. MORTAR. *(Rise.)* Why, I'd slap her hands!

KAREN. *(Ignoring Mrs. Mortar's speech. To Mary.)* Go upstairs, Mary.

MARY. I don't feel well.

KAREN. *(Sits in chair U.S. of desk. Wearily.)* Go upstairs, now.

MARY. I've got a pain. I've had it all morning. It hurts right here. *(Pointing vaguely in the direction of her heart.)* Really it does.

KAREN. Ask Miss Dobie to give you some hot water and bicarbonate of soda.

MARY. It's a bad pain. I've never had it before.

KAREN. *(Takes papers from desk, puts them in drawer.)* Go upstairs, Mary.

MARY. My heart! It's my heart! It's stopping or something. I can't breathe. *(She takes long breath and falls awkwardly to floor, her head upstage.)*

KAREN. *(Sighs, shakes head. To Mrs. Mortar.)* Ask Martha to phone Joe.

MRS. MORTAR. *(Crosses U.S. R. of desk. Looks at Mary.)* Do you think—? Heart trouble is very serious in a child. *(Exits U. C. Goes off L.)*

KAREN. *(Kneels beside her.)* Mary. Mary, get up. *(Karen crosses to L. of Mary, picks her up from floor, carries her off L. After a moment Martha Dobie enters through C. door from off L. She is about the same age as Karen. She is a nervous, high-strung woman. She pushes door shut behind her and puts two books she is carrying in bottom shelf of stage R. bookcase, gets pencil from a box as Karen enters from L. Karen, crossing to L. of desk.)* Did you get Joe?

MARTHA. *(Crossing to C., nodding.)* What happened to her? She was perfectly well a few hours ago.

KAREN. She still is. I told her she couldn't go to the boat-races and she decides to have a heart attack. *(Takes vase and flowers to cabinet U. L.)*

MARTHA. Where is she? *(Martha crosses to R. of desk.)*

KAREN. In there. Mortar's with her.

MARTHA. *(Takes exam papers from drawer of desk.)* Anything really wrong with her?

KAREN. I doubt it. *(Throws flowers into wastebasket R. of cabinet, comes back, sits down U.S. of desk, begins to mark papers.)* Isn't it wonderful what kids can think up? Her latest trick was kidding your aunt out of a lesson with those faded flowers we threw out. Then she threatened to go to her grandmother with some tale about being mistreated.

MARTHA. *(Sits in chair R. of desk.)* And, please God, Grandma would believe her and take her away from here. *(Karen gets cigarettes from desk drawer, offers one to Martha.)*

KAREN. No. But we ought to do something.

MARTHA. *(Takes cigarette.)* How about having a talk with Mrs. Tilford?

KAREN. *(Smiling.)* You want to do it?

MARTHA. *(Shakes head.)* No.

KAREN. I hate to do it. She's been so nice to us. *(Lights Martha's cigarette.)* Anyway, it wouldn't do any good. She's too crazy about Mary to see her clearly—and the kid knows it. *(Karen lights own cigarette.)*

MARTHA. How about asking Joe to say something to her? She'd listen to him. We don't get anywhere with Mary, and we might as well admit it. She's had more attention than any three kids put together. I am so bored with hearing myself say, "Mary, can I help you?" "Mary, are you worried about something?" Something goes on in that kid, and we don't know any more about it than we knew the first day she came. She causes trouble here. She's bad for the other girls. I don't know how or why, but it's wrong, and we must do something about it.

KAREN. I know. All right. We'll ask Joe what he thinks. Be nice if she didn't come back next term. *(Laughs.)* And be very nice if our other nuisance didn't come back, either.

MARTHA. *(Laughs.)* My aunt the actress? What's she been up to now?

KAREN. The usual foolishness. Last night at dinner she gave a full hour's lecture on the benefits of playing Cleopatra during a hurricane—that happened, she said, in Butte, Montana, on the night that a man in a box fell in love with her—he threw her a string of pearls.

MARTHA. I know the hurricane story. And sometimes the pearls are flowers and sometimes the man in the box is a duke, and once he was a king. I know all the stories.

KAREN. You must have had a gay childhood.,

MARTHA. *(Bitterly.)* Oh, I did. I did, indeed. How I used to hate all that—

KAREN. Couldn't we get rid of her soon, Martha? I don't want to make it hard on you, but she really ought not to be here.

MARTHA. *(After a moment.)* I know.

KAREN. We can scrape up enough money to send her away. Let's do it.

MARTHA. *(Affectionately pats her arm.)* You've been very patient about it. I'm sorry and I'll talk to her today. And I'll see to it that she goes soon.

KAREN. *(Looks at her watch.)* Did you get Joe himself on the phone?

MARTHA. He was already on his way. Isn't he always on his way over here? *(Corrects examination papers through next speeches.)*

KAREN. Well, I am going to marry him. I'm glad he wants to see me.

MARTHA. *(Slowly.)* You haven't talked about marriage for a long time. I mean, have you and Joe decided on—?

KAREN. Yes. We'll get married as soon as the term is over. We'll be out of debt by then and the school will be paying for itself. And Joe's found a house. We'll all go and look at it tomorrow

MARTHA. So soon? Then we won't be taking our vacation together?

KAREN. Of course we will. The three of us.

MARTHA. I had taken for granted, I guess, that we were going to the lake, like we always do, just you and I.

KAREN. Now there'll be three of us. That'll be fun, too.

MARTHA. Why haven't you told me this before?

KAREN. I'm not telling you anything we haven't talked about often.

MARTHA. You never told me that it was to be so soon. You never told me about a house or—

KAREN. We only decided the other night. *(Laughs.)* It's a big day for the school. I guess we're good teachers. Rosalie has finally put an "l" in could.

MARTHA. *(Rises, crosses R. below sofa to below R. end of sofa. In a dull, bitter tone.)* You really are going to leave, aren't you?

KAREN. I'm not going to leave, and you know it. Why do you say things like that? We agreed a long time ago that my marriage wasn't going to make any difference to the school.

MARTHA. But it will. You know it will. It can't help it.

KAREN. That's nonsense. Joe doesn't want me to give up here.

MARTHA. *(Moves up to R. end of sofa.)* I don't understand you. It's been so damned hard building this thing up, slaving and going without things to make ends meet—think of having a winter coat without holes in the lining again—and now when we're getting on our feet, you're all ready to let it go to hell.

KAREN. My marriage is not going to interfere with my work here. You're making something out of nothing.

MARTHA. *(Sits R. arm of sofa.)* It's going to be hard going on alone afterwards.

KAREN. *(Puts pencil down, rises. Gently.)* You haven't listened to a word I've said. You are not going on alone. You talk as if you had never taken the marriage very seriously.

MARTHA. I don't mean that, but it's so— *(Door U. C. opens, Dr. Joseph Cardin comes in. He is a large, pleasant-looking, carelessly dressed man of about thirty-five. He carries a doctor's bag, closes door behind him.)*

CARDIN. *(Goes to Karen. Kisses her.)* Hello, darling. Hi, Martha.

MARTHA. Hello, Joe.

KAREN. We tried to get you on the phone. Come in and look at your little cousin.

CARDIN. *(Laughs.)* I don't like to look at her much. What's the matter now? I stopped at Vernie's on my way over. Helped him with the new bull. Easier to deliver a baby—

KAREN. Come and see her. She says she has a pain in her heart. *(Crosses L. above desk. Exits L., leaving door open.)*

CARDIN. *(Crossing L. above desk.)* Our little Mary pops up in every day's dispatches.

MARTHA. *(Impatiently.)* Go and see her. Heart attacks are nothing to play with. *(Rises. Moves to D. R. table.)*

CARDIN. *(Looks at her.)* Never played with one in my life. *(Exits L. Martha sits in chair U. L. of D. R. table. Mrs. Mortar enters L., closing door, crosses above D. L. table to below desk.)*

MRS. MORTAR. *I* was asked to leave the room. *(Martha pays no attention.)* It seems that I'm not wanted in the room during the examination. It was a deliberate snub.

MARTHA. *(Over her shoulder.)* I don't think so.

MRS. MORTAR. *(Crosses to below R. end of sofa.)* I say it was a deliberate snub. Isn't it natural that the child should have me with her? Isn't it natural that an older woman should be present at a physical examination? *(No answer.)* Very well, if you are so thick-skinned that you don't resent these things— *(Sits R. end of sofa.)*

MARTHA. What are you talking about? Why in the name of heaven should you be with her?

MRS. MORTAR. I have been to good doctors in my better days. I say it's customary to have an older woman present.

MARTHA. *(Laughs.)* Tell that to Joe. Maybe he'll give you a job as duenna for his office.

MRS. MORTAR. *(Reminiscently.)* It was I who saved Delia Lampert's life the time she had that heart attack in Buffalo, right on the stage without losing a line. Poor Delia! She married Robert Laffonne in London after he found there was no soap with me. Not nine months later he left her and ran away with Eve Cloun, who had made a great hit playing the Infant Phenomenon when she was forty-seven, the British don't care about age. Delia's heart attack came afterwards—

MARTHA. *(Sharply.)* Yes. If you've seen one heart attack, you've seen them all.

MRS. MORTAR. So you don't resent your aunt being snubbed and humiliated?

MARTHA. Oh, Aunt Lily!

MRS. MORTAR. Karen is rude to me, and you know it.

MARTHA. *(Turns to Mrs. Mortar.)* I know that she is very kind to you, and—what's even harder—very patient.

MRS. MORTAR. Patient with me? I have worked my fingers to the bone to help you both—

MARTHA. *(Turns to papers.)* Don't tell yourself that too often, Aunt Lily; you'll come to believe it.

MRS. MORTAR. I know it's true. Where could you have gotten a woman of my reputation to give these children voice lessons, elocution lessons? Patient with me? Here I've donated my services—

MARTHA. You are being paid.

MRS. MORTAR. That small thing? I used to earn twice that for one performance.

MARTHA. No wonder the theater's in trouble. It was very extravagant of them to pay you so much. *(Suddenly tired of the whole thing.)* You've never been happy here, Aunt Lily.

MRS. MORTAR. Satisfied enough, I guess, for a poor relation.

MARTHA. You don't like the school or the farm or—

MRS. MORTAR. I told you at the beginning you shouldn't have bought a place like this. Burying yourself on a farm! Meeting no men! You'll regret it. *(Martha rises, taking papers with her. Crosses above sofa to L. of Mrs. Mortar.)*

MARTHA. We like it here. *(After a moment, leans over sofa to Mrs. Mortar.)* Aunt Lily, you've talked about London for a long time. Would you like to go over?

MRS. MORTAR. *(With a sigh.)* It's been twenty years. I shall never live to see it again.

MARTHA. You can go any time you like. We can spare the money now, and it will do you a lot of good. You pick out the boat and I'll get the passage. *(She has been talking rapidly, anxious to end the whole thing. Crosses L. to above desk.)* Now that's all fixed. You'll have a grand time seeing all your old friends, and if you live sensibly I ought to be able to let you have enough to get along on. *(Puts papers in desk drawer.)*

MRS. MORTAR. *(Slowly.)* So you want me to leave?

MARTHA. *(Gently.)* Aunt Lily, you've wanted to go ever since I can remember.

MRS. MORTAR. You're trying to get rid of me.

MARTHA. That's it. We don't want you around when we dig up the buried treasure.

MRS. MORTAR. So? You're turning me out? At my age! Nice, grateful girl you are!

MARTHA. *(Angrily, crosses to below L. end of sofa.)* How can anybody deal with you? You're going where you want to go, and we'll be better off alone. That suits everybody. You complain about the

20

farm, you complain about the school, you complain about Karen, and now you have what you want and you're still looking for something to complain about.

MRS. MORTAR. *(Rises. With dignity.)* Please do not raise your voice.

MARTHA. Be glad I don't do worse.

MRS. MORTAR. I'm not going to England. I refuse to let you ship me off any place you like. I shall go back to the stage. I'll write to my agents tomorrow, and just as soon as they have something for me I'll be out of here. *(Moves away R.)*

MARTHA. The truth is I'd like you to leave soon. We can't live together, and it doesn't make any difference whose fault it is.

MRS. MORTAR. *(Turns to Martha.)* You wish me to go tonight?

MARTHA. Oh, stop it, Aunt Lily. *(Moves up C.)* Go as soon as you've found a place you like. I'll put the money in the bank for you tomorrow.

MRS. MORTAR. You think I'd take your money? I'd rather scrub floors first.

MARTHA. You'll change your mind after the first floor. *(Crosses to below desk.)* I've done the best I could by you for years, Aunt Lily. Your coming here wasn't ever thought of as a permanent arrangement. You knew that. You'll be happier—

MRS. MORTAR. *(Laughs knowingly. Moves up to R. of sofa.)* I should have known by this time that the wise thing is to stay out of your way when he's in the house.

MARTHA. What are you talking about now?

MRS. MORTAR. *(Crosses D. R.)* Never mind. I should have known better. You always take your spite out on me.

MARTHA. Spite? *(Crosses up R. of desk to above desk. Impatiently.)* Oh, don't let's have any more of this today. I'm tired. I've been working since six o'clock this morning.

MRS. MORTAR. Any day that he's in the house is a bad day.

MARTHA. *(Crosses to C.)* When *who* is in the house?

MRS. MORTAR. *(Crosses up to R. of sofa.)* Don't think you're fooling me, young lady. I wasn't born yesterday. And I didn't meet you last month.

MARTHA. *(Crosses R. to above C. of sofa.)* I don't know what you're talking about. But I do know that the amount of disconnected nonsense in your head tires me, and always has. Now go take your nap.

MRS. MORTAR. *(Crosses to Martha.)* I know what I know. Every time that man comes into this house, you're in a bad humor. *(Crosses*

21

L. upstage of Martha to above chair R. of desk.) It seems like you just can't stand the idea of them being together. God knows what you'll do when they get married. You're jealous, that's what it is.

MARTHA. *(Her voice is tense and previous attitude of good-natured irritation is gone, turns to Mrs. Mortar.)* I'm very fond of Joe, and you know it.

MRS. MORTAR. *(Crossing to C.)* I don't know who you're fond of. I've never understood you. *(Martha moves away upstage.)* You'd better get a beau of your own. That's what you need. Every woman, no matter what she says, is jealous when another woman gets a husband. You'd just better set your cap for what comes along now—

MARTHA. *(Comes back to above L. end of sofa. Very sharply.)* Aunt Lily, please stop that talk. I had too much of it for too many years. I can't take any more.

MRS. MORTAR. *(Crosses to Martha.)* You've always had a jealous and possessive nature. Even as a child. *(Martha turns away.)* If you had a friend, you always got mad if she liked anybody else. That's what's happening now. And it's unnatural. Just as unnatural as it can be. I say you need a man of your own, and—

MARTHA. *(Turns to Mrs. Mortar.)* The sooner you get out of here, the better. You are making me sick and I won't stand for you any longer. I want you to leave. And now. I don't wish any delay about it— *(At this point there is a sound outside C. door. Martha breaks off, angry and ashamed. Mrs. Mortar crosses L. to above chair R. of desk. After a moment, Martha crosses to door, opens it. Evelyn and Peggy are seen on staircase, Peggy is picking up some books she has dropped. For a second Martha stands still as they stop and look at her. Then, afraid that her anger with her aunt will color anything she might say to the children, she crosses to above L. end of sofa and stands with her back to them.)* What were you doing outside the door? *(Evelyn and Peggy enter room.)*

EVELYN. *(L. C. Hurriedly.)* We were going upstairs, Miss Dobie.

PEGGY. *(R. C.)* We came down to see how Mary was.

MARTHA. And you stopped long enough to see how we were? Did you deliberately listen?

PEGGY. We didn't mean to. We heard voices and we couldn't help—

MRS. MORTAR. *(Fake social tone.)* Eavesdropping is something ladies just don't do.

MARTHA. *(Turning to face the children.)* Go upstairs now. We'll talk about this later. *(Slowly shuts door as they begin to climb stairs.)*

MRS. MORTAR. You mean to say you're not going to do anything about that?

MARTHA. *(Thoughtfully.)* You should not be around children.

MRS. MORTAR. What exactly does that mean?

MARTHA. *(Crosses down to L. end of sofa.)* This is their home, and things shouldn't be said in it that they can't hear. When you're at your best, you're not for tender ears.

MRS. MORTAR. *(Crosses to C.)* So now it's my fault, is it? You'd better start looking at yourself, and not bother so much with me— *(L. door opens and Cardin comes in, crossing to L. of desk.)* Good day, Joseph. *(Mrs. Mortar, head in air, gives Martha a malicious half-smile and makes what she thinks is a majestic exit U. C., closing door.)*

MARTHA. How is Mary?

CARDIN. *(Puts his bag on desk, puts away his stethoscope.)* What's the matter with the Duchess? *(Nods at door C.)*

MARTHA. Rehearsing an exit in case she finds the right play. What about Mary?

CARDIN. Nothing.

MARTHA. *(Sighs.)* I thought so.

CARDIN. *(Laughs.)* Just a little something she thought up. Heart trouble sounds important, and I guess she'd heard somewhere that fainting scares people.

MARTHA. *(Crosses L., leans against downstage side of desk.)* But it's such a silly thing to do. She knew we'd have you in. *(Sighs.)* Maybe she's not as bright as we think she is. Any idiots in your family, Joe? Any inbreeding?

CARDIN. *(Sits in chair L. of desk.)* Don't blame her on me. It's another side of the family. *(Laughs.)* I don't want any part of her.

MARTHA. Look, Joe, have you any idea what is the matter with Mary? I mean, has she always been like this?

CARDIN. She's always been a honey. And her grandmother's spoiling hasn't helped any, either. Her father was Aunt Amelia's favorite son. God knows why, but—

MARTHA. We're reaching the end of our rope with her. This kind of thing can't go on.

CARDIN. *(Looking at her.)* Aren't you taking it too seriously? *(Lights cigarette.)*

MARTHA. *(After a second.)* I guess I am. But you stay around kids long enough and you won't know what to take seriously, either. But I do think somebody ought to talk to Mrs. Tilford about her.

CARDIN. *(Laughs.)* You wouldn't be meaning me now, would you?

MARTHA. Well, she is your aunt and Karen and I were talking about it this afternoon and—

CARDIN. I'm marrying Karen but I am not going to write Mary Tilford into the contract. Incidentally, Karen tell you we're thinking of the old King house that's up for sale?

MARTHA. *(Sharply.)* She told me. Incidentally.

CARDIN. What's the matter, Martha?

MARTHA. Nothing.

CARDIN. *(His face is grave, his voice gentle.)* Yes, there is. For a long time you and I have had something to talk about. Every time I speak of marrying Karen— *(Martha turns away slightly. He rises, goes to her.)* Look here, I'm very fond of you and I've always thought you liked me. *(Turns her to him.)* Don't worry about the school. I don't want her to leave here, it isn't going to be like that. She'll still be with you here—

MARTHA. *(Pushes his hands away.)* Damn you! Leave me alone. Stop consoling me or patronizing me or feeling sorry for me or whatever you're doing. Leave me alone— *(Puts her face in her hands. Cardin watches her in silence, then goes to D. L. table, puts out his cigarette. When she takes her hands from her face, she holds them out to him, crosses to him. Contritely.)* Joe, please, I'm sorry. I don't know what's got into me. I'm turning into a nasty, bitter—

CARDIN. *(Takes her hands in one of his, patting them with his other hand.)* You're not turning into anything except the nice woman you are. *(Puts an arm around her, and she leans her head against his lapel. They are standing like that when Karen comes in L.)*

MARTHA. *(To Karen, as she wipes her eyes.)* Your friend's got a nice shoulder to weep on. *(Crosses R. to above L. end of sofa.)*

KAREN. *(Has crossed to R. of Cardin, puts her arms around him.)* He's an admirable man in every way. Well, the angel child is now looking very hurt and putting her clothes back on.

MARTHA. Her influence is abroad even while she's unconscious. Her roommates were busy listening at the door while Aunt Lily and I were yelling at each other.

KAREN. We'll have to move those girls away from one another. Away from Mary. *(School bell rings from rear of the house.)*

MARTHA. That's my class. I'll send Peggy and Evelyn down. Better put them in another room.

KAREN. Yes, I will. *(Martha exits C., leaving door open. She goes up*

stairs. Karen goes toward L. door. Cardin sits in D. L. chair.) Mary!
Mary! *(Mary opens door, comes in, stands above chair L. of desk, buttoning neck of her dress. Karen moves R. above desk to above chair L. of desk.)*

CARDIN. *(To Mary.)* How's it feel to be back from the grave? Meet any interesting people?

MARY. My heart hurts.

CARDIN. *(Laughing.)* You like that story, don't you?

MARY. It's my heart, and it hurts. I want to see my grandmother. I want to— *(Evelyn and Peggy timidly come downstairs and enter C.)*

KAREN. Come in, girls, I want to talk to you.

PEGGY. *(L. C.)* We're awfully sorry, really. We just didn't think and—

KAREN. I'm sorry, too, Peggy. *(Thoughtfully.)* You and Evelyn never used to do things like this. We'll have to separate you three.

EVELYN. *(Above L. end of sofa.)* Ah, Miss Wright, we've been together almost a year.

KAREN. It was evidently too long. Peggy, you will move into Lois' room, and Lois will move in with Evelyn. Mary will go in with Rosalie.

MARY. Rosalie hates me.

KAREN. That's a silly thing to say. I can't imagine Rosalie hating anyone.

MARY. *(Starting to cry.)* And it's all because I had a pain. If anybody else was sick they'd be put to bed and petted. You're always mean to me. I get blamed and punished for everything. *(To Cardin.)* I do, Cousin Joe. All the time for everything. *(Mary by now is crying violently and as Karen half moves toward her, Cardin, who has been frowning, picks Mary up and puts her down on sofa. Evelyn moves R. above sofa. Peggy moves up to bookcase L. of C. door.)*

CARDIN. *(Sits beside Mary on sofa.)* You've been unpleasant enough to Miss Wright. Lie here until you've stopped working yourself into a fit. Come over to the office one day. I'll show you how to do a good faint. *(Crosses to desk, picks up his bag, smiles at Karen.)* She's not going to hurt herself crying. *(Crosses upstage between sofa and desk, he reaches over, pats Mary's head.)* Take good care of yourself. *(Exits C.)*

KAREN. I'll walk to the car with you. *(To girls.)* Go up now and move your things. Tell Lois to get her stuff ready. *(Exits C. A second after they leave, Mary springs up, throws a cushion from sofa at door.)*

EVELYN. *(Closing door.)* Don't do that. She'll hear you. *(Peggy picks up cushion, puts it back on sofa.)*

MARY. Who cares if she does? And she can hear that, too. *(Takes small china kitchen ornament, a kitten, from table and throws it on floor. Evelyn and Peggy gasp, and Mary's bravado disappears for a moment. She rises.)*

EVELYN. *(Frightened.)* Now what are you going to do?

PEGGY. *(Stooping down to pick up the pieces. Evelyn helps her.)* You'll get the devil now. Dr. Cardin gave it to Miss Wright. It was a lover's gift. There's nothing like a lover's gift. *(They put pieces on desk. Peggy sits in chair R. of desk. Evelyn gets some scotch tape from lower shelf of the stage L. bookcase, comes to upstage of desk. Together they try to fix kitten.)*

MARY. Oh, leave it alone. She'll never know we did it.

PEGGY. *We* didn't do it. *You* did it.

MARY. And what will you do if I say *we* did do it? *(Coughs. Sits on sofa and balances cushion on her head.)* Never mind, I'll think of something else. The wind could've knocked it over.

EVELYN. Yeh. She's going to believe that one!

MARY. Oh, stop worrying about it. I'll get out of it. *(Puts pillow down.)*

EVELYN. Did you really have a pain?

MARY. I fainted, didn't I?

PEGGY. I wish I could faint. Is it hard? I've never even worn glasses, or braces, and I've got my own tonsils.

MARY. A lot it'll get you to faint.

EVELYN. What did Miss Wright do to you when the class left?

MARY. Told me I couldn't go to the boat-races.

EVELYN. *(Sits on R. down side of chair upstage of desk.)* Gosh…

PEGGY. But we'll tell you everything that happens and we'll give you all the souvenirs and things.

MARY. I won't let you go if I can't go. But I'll find some way to go. What was she talking about when she moved you? What were *you* doing?

PEGGY. We came down to see what was happening to you, but the doors were closed and we could hear Miss Dobie and Mortar having an awful row. Then Miss Dobie opens the door and there we were.

MARY. And a lot of crawling and crying you both did too, I bet.

EVELYN. We were sort of sorry about listening. I guess it wasn't—

MARY. Ah, you're always sorry about everything. What were they saying?

PEGGY. What was who saying?

MARY. Dobie and Mortar, silly.

PEGGY. *(Evasively.)* Just talking, I guess.

EVELYN. Fighting.

MARY. About what?

EVELYN. Well, they were talking about Mortar going away to England and—

PEGGY. *(To Evelyn.)* You know, it really wasn't very nice to've listened, and I think maybe it's worse to tell.

MARY. *(Rises, crosses upstage between sofa and desk to R. of Evelyn.)* You do, do you? You just don't tell me and see what happens. *(Peggy sighs.)*

EVELYN. Mortar got awful sore at that and said they just wanted to get rid of her, and then they started talking about Dr. Cardin.

MARY. What about him?

PEGGY. We'd better get started moving; Miss Wright will be back first thing we know.

MARY. *(Fiercely.)* Shut up! *(Pokes Evelyn.)* Go on, Evelyn.

EVELYN. They're going to be married. The two of them.

MARY. *(Crosses R. to above R. end of sofa.)* Everybody knows that.

PEGGY. But everybody doesn't know that Miss Dobie doesn't want them to get married. How do you like that? *(C. door opens. Rosalie Wells sticks her head in.)*

ROSALIE. I have a class soon. If you're going to move your things—

MARY. Close that door, you idiot. *(Rosalie closes door, stands near it.)* What do you want?

ROSALIE. *(Crosses to Mary.)* I'm trying to tell you. If you're going to move your things—not that I want you in with me, the devil knows—you'd better start right now. Miss Wright's coming in a minute.

MARY. *(Sits back of sofa.)* Who cares if she is?

ROSALIE. I'm just telling you for your own good, the devil knows.

PEGGY. *(Starts to get up.)* We're coming.

MARY. No. Let Rosalie move our things.

ROSALIE. You crazy? *(Voice mounts.)*

PEGGY. *(Rises, crosses L. below desk. Nervously.)* It's all right. Evelyn and I'll get your things. Come on, Evelyn.

MARY. Trying to get out of telling me, huh? Well, you won't get out of it that way. Sit down and stop being such a sissy. *(Peggy crosses U. L. of desk, sits on L. arm of chair upstage of desk.)* Rosalie, tell

27

you what, you go on up and move my things and don't say a word about our being down here.

ROSALIE. And who was your French maid yesterday, Mary Tilford? And who will wait upon you in the insane asylum?

MARY. *(Laughing.)* You'll do for today. *(Picks cushion up from sofa, hits Rosalie with it. Rosalie backs away.)* Now go on, Rosalie, and fix our things.

ROSALIE. You crazy?

MARY. And the next time we go into town I'll let you wear my gold beads and my pearl pin. You'll like that, won't you, Rosalie?

ROSALIE. *(Draws back, moves her hands nervously.)* I don't know what you're talking about, the devil knows.

MARY. Oh, I'm not talking about anything in particular. You just run along now and remind me the next time to lend you—*lend* you—my beads and pin.

ROSALIE. *(Stares at her a moment. Slowly crosses toward Mary.)* All right, I'll do it this time, but just 'cause I got a good disposition. But don't think you're going to boss me around, Mary Tilford.

MARY. *(Smiling.)* No, indeed. *(Rosalie goes to C. door, opens it. Mary follows her.)* And get the things done neatly, Rosalie. Don't muss my white blouse. *(Rosalie exits slamming door as Mary laughs, opens door, calls after her.)* My tennis shoes need cleaning.

EVELYN. Now what do you think of that? What made her so agreeable?

MARY. *(Closes door, crosses downstage, sits in chair R. of desk.)* Oh, a little secret we got. Go on, now, what else did she say?

PEGGY. Well, Mortar said that Dobie was jealous of them, and that she was like that when she was a little girl, and that she'd better get herself a beau of her own because it was unnatural, and that she never wanted anybody to like Miss Wright, and that was unnatural. Boy! Did Miss Dobie get sore at that!

EVELYN. Then we didn't hear any more. Peggy dropped some books.

MARY. What'd she mean Dobie was jealous?

PEGGY. What's unnatural?

EVELYN. Un for not. Not natural.

PEGGY. It's funny, because everybody gets married.

MARY. A lot of people don't—they're too ugly.

PEGGY. *(Claps hand to her mouth.)* Oh, my God! Rosalie'll find that copy of *Mademoiselle de Maupin*. She'll blab like the dickens.

MARY. Ah, she won't say a word.

EVELYN. *(Leans toward Mary.)* Who gets the book when we move?
MARY. You can have it. That's what I was doing this morning—finishing it. There's one part in it—
PEGGY. What part? *(Mary laughs.)*
EVELYN. Well, what was it?
MARY. Wait until you read it.
EVELYN. Did you understand it? I don't always—
PEGGY. It's a shame about being moved. I don't want to go in with Helen: she's John's cousin, you know, and I don't want to talk about the whole thing.
EVELYN. What whole thing? You've only met him once.
MARY. It was a dirty trick making us move. She just wants to see how much fun she can take away from me. She hates me.
PEGGY. No, she doesn't, Mary. She treats you just like the rest of us—almost better.
MARY. That's right, stick up for your crush. Take her side against mine.
PEGGY. I didn't mean it that way.
EVELYN. *(Looks at her watch. Rises.)* We'd better get upstairs.
MARY. I'm not going.
PEGGY. Rosalie isn't so bad.
EVELYN. What you going to do about the kitten?
MARY. I don't care about Rosalie and I don't care about the kitten. *(Mary grabs what is left of kitten. Peggy and Evelyn take it away from her.)* I'm not going to be here.
PEGGY. Not going to be here!
EVELYN. What do you mean?
MARY. *(Calmly.)* I'm going home.
PEGGY. Oh, Mary—
EVELYN. You can't do that.
MARY. Oh, can't I? You just watch. I'm not staying here. *(Rises, slowly crosses L. below desk to U. L. of chair L. of desk.)* I'm going home and tell Grandma I'm not staying anymore. *(Smiles to herself.)* I'll tell her I'm not happy. They're scared of Grandma—she helped 'em when they first started, you know—and when she tells 'em something, believe me, they'll sit up and listen. They can't get away with treating me like this, and they don't have to think they can.
PEGGY. *(Appalled.)* You just going to walk out like that?
EVELYN. What you going to tell your grandmother?
MARY. Oh, who cares? I'll think of something to tell her. I can always do it better on the spur of the moment.

PEGGY. *(Rises.)* She'll send you right back.

MARY. *(Crosses to down L. table, fingers lamp.)* You let me worry about that. Grandma's very fond of me, on account my father was her favorite son. My father killed himself, but Grandma won't admit it. I can manage her all right.

PEGGY. I don't think you ought to go, really, Mary. It's just going to make an awful lot of trouble.

EVELYN. What's going to happen about the kitten?

MARY. Say I did it—it doesn't make a bit of difference anymore to me. *(Crosses back to U. L. of chair, L. of desk.)* Now listen, you two got to help. They won't miss me before dinner if you make Rosalie shut the door and keep it shut. Now, I'll go through the field to French's, and then I can get the bus to Homestead.

EVELYN. How you going to get to the street car?

MARY. Taxi, idiot.

PEGGY. How are you going to get out of here in the first place?

MARY. *(Slowly moving downstage.)* I'm going to walk out. I know where they keep the front door. Well, I'm going right out the door.

EVELYN. Gee, I wouldn't have the nerve.

MARY. Of course you wouldn't. You'd let 'em do anything to you they want. Well, they can't do it to me. *(Turns to them.)* Who's got any money? *(Peggy slowly crosses R. above desk, comes downstage between sofa and desk to below L. end of sofa.)*

EVELYN. *(Moves to above chair R. of desk.)* Not me. Not a cent. Not a cent.

MARY. I've got to have a dollar for the taxi and a dime for the bus.

EVELYN. And where you going to find it?

PEGGY. *(Below L. end of sofa.)* See? Why don't you just wait until you get your allowance on Monday, and then you can go any place you want. Maybe by that time—

MARY. I'm going today. *Now.*

EVELYN. You can't *walk* to Lancet.

MARY. *(Slowly crosses R. below desk to C. To Peggy.)* You've got money. You've got three dollars and twenty-five cents. Go get it for me.

PEGGY. *(Moves away R. below sofa.)* No! No! I won't get it for you.

EVELYN. *(Crosses to C.)* You can't have that money, Mary—

MARY. *(Advances to below L. end of sofa.)* Get it for me.

PEGGY. *(Cringes, her voice is scared.)* I won't. I just won't. Mamma doesn't send me much allowance—not half as much as the rest of you get—I saved this so long—you took it from me last time—

30

EVELYN. *(Comes down L. of Mary.)* Ah, she wants that dress so bad.
PEGGY. I'll tell you a secret. I'd never even go to the movies if Miss Wright and Miss Dobie didn't give me money. I never have anything the rest of you get all the time. It took me so long to save that and—
MARY. Go upstairs and get me the money.
PEGGY. *(Hysterically, backing away from her.)* I won't. I won't. I won't. *(Mary makes a sudden move to her, grabs her L. arm, and jerks it back, hard and expertly. Peggy screams softly. Evelyn tries to take Mary's arm away. Without releasing her hold on Peggy, Mary slaps Evelyn's face. Evelyn backs away, begins to cry.)*
MARY. Just say when you've had enough.
PEGGY. *(Softly, stiflingly.)* All—all right—I'll get it.
MARY. *(Smiles, nods her head, releases Peggy, softly.)* Go on, go on. *(Peggy, crying and rubbing her arm, slowly crosses U. C. toward door as* CURTAIN FALLS.*)*

ACT II

Scene 1

SCENE: *Living room at Mrs. Tilford's. It is a formal room, without being cold or elegant. The furniture is old, but excellent.*

On the stage R. wall are two sconces, between which stands a highboy. On each side of highboy is a Chippendale chair. In up right corner of room is a tall wooden pedestal, on which is a silver champagne bucket with flowers. Stage R., against upstage wall, is a large sideboard. On the sideboard: on each end a large glass hurricane lamp with candle; in C. a large china bowl with flowers; R. of the china bowl, a bowl of fruit and a dish lof nuts and chocolate; L. of china bowl, a small silver tray with three highball glasses, two bottles of liquor, and pitcher of water. Hanging on wall over sideboard is a large oval oil painting of a Venetian scene. To L. of sideboard is a wide arch with gold drapes. On either side of arch, hung one above the other, are three glass silhouettes. L. of arch is a small half-round console table flanked by two Chippendale chairs. On table: a phone and a large silver lamp. Upstage of arch, a hall which leads, L., to front door, and, R., into house. A chandelier hangs in C. of hall. Against back wall of hall is another half-round console table, on which is a large tea box. On wall over table is an oil painting. To R. of table, a side chair. R. C. of room is a love seat with small pillows at each end. D. R. of love seat, an ottoman with a swivel seat. L. of love seat is a small table and a wooden armchair. L. C. an identical love seat and pillows, with a coffee table in front of it. There are cigarette boxes and ashtrays on both tables. Entrances D. R. and D. L. just above the portal line.

AT RISE: *Stage is empty. Voices are heard in hall.*

AGATHA. *(Off L.)* What are *you* doing here? Well, come on in—don't stand there gaping at me. Have they given you a holiday or did you just decide you'd get a better dinner here? *(Mary enters through arch, followed by Agatha. Agatha is a sharp-faced maid, no longer young, with a querulous voice.)* Can't you even say hello?

MARY. *(Throws her coat on chair L. of desk, lies on L. love seat with her feet on R. end.)* Hello, Agatha. You didn't give me a chance. Where's Grandma?

AGATHA. *(Comes down to R. of L. love seat, pushes Mary's feet off.)* Why aren't you in school? Look at your face and clothes. Where have you been?

MARY. I got a little dirty coming home. I walked part of the way through the woods.

AGATHA. Then why didn't you wear your old brown coat?

MARY. Oh, stop asking me questions. Where's Grandma?

AGATHA. *(Moves to upstage of love seat.)* Where ought any clean person be at this time of day? She's taking a bath.

MARY. Is anybody coming for dinner?

AGATHA. She didn't say anything about you coming.

MARY. How could she? She didn't know.

AGATHA. *(Crosses to above R. end of love seat, leans over it to Mary.)* Then what are you doing here?

MARY. *(Quickly sits on R. end of love seat.)* Leave me alone. I don't feel well.

AGATHA. Why don't you feel well? Who ever heard of a person going for a walk in the woods when they didn't feel well?

MARY. Oh, leave me alone. I came home because I was sick.

AGATHA. You look all right.

MARY. But I don't feel all right. *(Whining.)* I can't even come home without everybody nagging at me.

AGATHA. Don't think you're fooling me, young lady. You might pull the wool over some people's eyes, but—I bet you've been up to something again. *(Stares suspiciously at Mary, who says nothing.)* Well, you wait right here till I tell your grandmother. And if you feel so sick, you certainly don't want any dinner. A good dose of rhubarb and soda will fix you up. *(Exits through arch, goes off R. Mary makes a face in direction Agatha has gone, stops sniffling. She looks nervously around the room, then rises, rubs her shoes against her legs to clean them, crosses up to sideboard. She quickly eats some grapes, then tries to rub some of dirt from her face. Mrs. Tilford, followed by*

Agatha, enters through arch from off R. Mrs. Tilford is a large, dignified woman in her sixties, with a pleasant, strong face. Agatha, offstage to Mrs. Tilford, as she follows her into room:) Why didn't you put some cold water on your chest? Do you want to catch your death of cold at your age? Did you have to hurry so? *(She crosses to above L. end of L. love seat.)*

MARY. Grandma!

MRS. TILFORD. *(U. C.)* Mary, what are you doing home? *(Mary rushes to her and buries her head in Mrs. Tilford's dress, crying. Mrs. Tilford lets her cry for a moment while she pats her head and puts arm around her.)* Never mind, dear; now stop crying and tell me what is the matter.

MARY. *(Gradually stops crying, fondling Mrs. Tilford's hand, playing on the older woman's affection for her.)* It's so good to see you, Grandma. You didn't come to visit me all last week.

MRS. TILFORD. I couldn't, dear. But I was coming tomorrow.

MARY. I missed you so. *(Smiling up at Mrs. Tilford.)* I was awful homesick.

MRS. TILFORD. *(Leads Mary down C.)* I'm glad that's all it was. I was frightened when Agatha said you were not well.

AGATHA. Did I say that? I said she only came home for Wednesday night fudge cake. *(Mary crosses below Mrs. Tilford to in front of L. love seat.)*

MRS. TILFORD. But how did you get here? Did Miss Karen drive you over?

MARY. I—I walked most of the way, and then a lady gave me a ride and— *(Looks timidly at Mrs. Tilford.)*

AGATHA. Did she have to walk through the woods in her very best coat?

MRS. TILFORD. Mary! Do you mean you left without permission?

MARY. *(Nervously.)* I ran away, Grandma. They didn't know—

MRS. TILFORD. That was a very bad thing to do, and they'll be worried. Agatha, phone Miss Wright and tell her Mary is here. John will drive her back before dinner.

MARY. *(As Agatha starts toward phone.)* No. Grandma, don't do that. Please don't do that. Please let me stay.

MRS. TILFORD. But, darling, you can't leave school any time you please.

MARY. Oh, please, Grandma, don't send me back right away. You don't know how they'll punish me.

MRS. TILFORD. *(Sits on R. end of L. love seat.)* I don't think they'll be that angry. Come, you're acting like a foolish little girl.

MARY. *(Hysterically, as she sees Agatha about to pick up phone.)* Grandma! Please! I can't go back! I can't! They'll kill me! They will, Grandma! They'll kill me! *(Mrs. Tilford and Agatha stare at Mary in amazement. She sits beside Mrs. Tilford, puts her arm through hers, leans against her and sobs.)*

MRS. TILFORD. *(Motioning with a hand for Agatha to leave the room.)* Never mind phoning now, Agatha.

AGATHA. If you're going to let her— *(Mrs. Tilford repeats gesture. Agatha picks up Mary's coat, exits down L., with offended dignity.)*

MRS. TILFORD. Stop crying, Mary.

MARY. It's so nice here, Grandma.

MRS. TILFORD. I'm glad you like being home with me, but at your age you can hardly— *(More seriously.)* What made you talk that way about Miss Wright and Miss Dobie? You can't say such things about people, Mary. You know very well they wouldn't hurt you for anything.

MARY. Oh, but they would. They—I— *(Breaks off, looks around as if hunting for a clue to her next word, then dramatically.)* I fainted today.

MRS. TILFORD. *(Alarmed.)* Fainted?

MARY. Yes, I did. My heart—I had a pain in my heart. I couldn't help having a pain in my heart, and when I fainted right in class, they called Cousin Joe and he said I didn't. He said it was maybe only that I ate my breakfast too fast and Miss Wright blamed me for it.

MRS. TILFORD. *(Relieved.)* If Joseph said it wasn't serious, it wasn't.

MARY. But I did have a pain in my heart—honest.

MRS. TILFORD. Have you still got it?

MARY. I guess I haven't got it much anymore, but I feel a little weak, and I was scared of Miss Wright being so mean to me just because I was sick.

MRS. TILFORD. Scared of Karen? Nonsense. It's perfectly possible that you had a pain, but if you had really been sick Joseph would certainly have known it. It's not nice to frighten people by pretending to be more sick than you are.

MARY. I didn't *want* to be sick, but I'm always getting punished for everything.

MRS. TILFORD. *(Gently.)* You mustn't imagine things like that, child, or you'll grow up to be a very unhappy woman. I'm not going to scold you any more for coming home this time, though I suppose I should. Run along upstairs and wash your face, and change your dress, and after dinner John will drive you back. Run along.

MARY. *(Rises. Happily.)* I can stay for dinner?

MRS. TILFORD. Yes.

MARY. *(Slowly crosses U. L. of love seat.)* Maybe I could stay till the first of the week. Saturday's your birthday and I could be here with you.

MRS. TILFORD. We won't celebrate my birthday, dear. We'll wait for yours. You'll go back to school after dinner.

MARY. But— *(She hesitates, then goes to back of love seat and puts her arms around the older woman's neck. Softly:)* How much do you love me?

MRS. TILFORD. *(Smiling.)* As much as all the words in all the books in all the world.

MARY. Remember when I was little and you used to tell me that right before I went to sleep? And it was a rule nobody could say another single word after you finished? You used to say: "Wor-rr-ld," and then I had to shut my eyes tight. I miss you an awful lot, Grandma.

MRS. TILFORD. And I miss you, but I'm afraid my Latin is rusty—you'll do better in school.

MARY. *(Moves to above L. end of love seat.)* But couldn't I stay out the rest of this term? After the summer maybe I won't mind it so much. I'll study hard, honest, by myself, and—

MRS. TILFORD. Don't be silly, Mary. Back you go tonight. Let's not have any more talk about it now, and let's have no more— running away from school ever.

MARY. *(Slowly.)* Then I really have to go back there tonight?

MRS. TILFORD. Of course you do.

MARY. *(Comes down to below L. end of love seat.)* You don't love me. You don't care whether they kill me or not.

MRS. TILFORD. Mary!

MARY. You don't! You don't! You don't care what happens to me.

MRS. TILFORD. *(Rises. Sternly.)* But I *do* care that you're talking this way.

MARY. *(Meekly.)* I'm sorry I said that, Grandma. I didn't mean to hurt your feelings. *(Crosses to Mrs. Tilford, puts arms around her.)* Forgive me?

MRS. TILFORD. What made you talk like that?

MARY. *(In a whisper.)* I'm scared, Grandma, I'm scared. They'll do dreadful things to me.

MRS. TILFORD. Dreadful? Nonsense. They'll punish you for running away. You deserve to be punished.

MARY. *(Sits L. end of love seat.)* It's not that. It's not anything I do. It never is. They—they punish me, anyhow, just like they got something against me. I'm afraid of them, Grandma, and that's the truth.

MRS. TILFORD. *(Sits beside her.)* I've never heard such nonsense. What have they ever done to you that is so terrible?

MARY. A lot of things—all the time. Miss Wright says I can't go to the boat-races and— *(Realizing the inadequacy of this reply, she breaks off, hesitates, hunting for a more telling reply, and finally stammers.)* It's—it's after what happened today.

MRS. TILFORD. You mean something else besides your naughtiness in pretending to faint and then running away?

MARY. I *did* faint. I didn't pretend. They just said that to make me feel bad. Anyway, it wasn't anything that I did.

MRS. TILFORD. What was it, then?

MARY. I can't tell you.

MRS. TILFORD. Why?

MARY. *(Sulkily.)* Because you're just going to take their part.

MRS. TILFORD. *(A little annoyed.)* Very well. Now run upstairs and get ready for dinner.

MARY. It was—it was all about Miss Dobie and Mrs. Mortar. They were talking awful things, and Peggy and Evelyn heard them and Miss Dobie found out, and then they made us move our rooms.

MRS. TILFORD. What has that to do with you? I don't understand what you're talking about.

MARY. They made us move our rooms. They said we couldn't be together anymore. And they have a good reason. They're afraid to have us near them, that's what it is, and they're taking it out on me. They're scared of you.

MRS. TILFORD. You're talking like a crazy girl. Why should they be scared of me? Am I such an unpleasant old lady?

MARY. They're afraid you'll find out.

MRS. TILFORD. Find out what?

MARY. *(Vaguely.)* Things.

MRS. TILFORD. You're talking gibberish. Now run along before I get angry.

MARY. All right. But there're a lot of things. They have secrets, and they're afraid I'll find out and tell you.

MRS. TILFORD. There's nothing wrong with people having secrets.

MARY. But they've got funny ones. Peggy and Evelyn heard Mrs. Mortar telling Miss Dobie that she was jealous of Miss Wright marrying Cousin Joe.

MRS. TILFORD. You shouldn't repeat things like that. It means nothing and—

MARY. She said it was unnatural for a girl to feel that way. *(Rises, crosses up around L. end of love seat and R. to R. of love seat.)* That's what she said, Grandma. *(Mrs. Tilford turns her head.)* I'm just telling you what she said. She said there was something funny about it, and that Miss Dobie had always been like that, even when she was a little girl and that it was unnatural—

MRS. TILFORD. Stop using that silly word, Mary.

MARY. *(Vaguely realizing that she is on the right track, hurries on. She moves downstage to below R. love seat, sits on L. end.)* But that was the word *she* kept using, Grandma, and then Miss Dobie got mad and told Mrs. Mortar she'd have to get out of the house.

MRS. TILFORD. That was probably not the reason at all.

MARY. *(Nodding vigorously.)* I bet it was, because honestly, Miss Dobie does get cranky and mean every time Cousin Joe comes, and today I heard her say to him: "Damn you," and then she said she was just a jealous fool and he was to leave her alone and—

MRS. TILFORD. *(Rises.)* You have picked up some very fine words, haven't you, Mary?

MARY. That's just what she said, Grandma, and one time Miss Dobie was crying in Miss Wright's room, and Miss Wright was trying to stop her, and she said that all right, maybe she wouldn't get married right away if—

MRS. TILFORD. *(Crosses R. to R. of armchair.)* How do you know all this?

MARY. We couldn't help hearing because they—I mean Miss Dobie was talking awful loud, and their room is right next to ours.

MRS. TILFORD. *(Sits in armchair.)* Whose room?

MARY. Miss Wright's room, I mean, and you can just ask Peggy and Evelyn whether we didn't hear. Almost always Miss Dobie comes in after we go to bed and stays a long time. I guess that's why they want to get rid of us—of me—because we hear things. That's why they're making us move our room, and they punish me all the time for—

MRS. TILFORD. For eavesdropping, I should think. *(She has said this mechanically. With nothing definite in her mind, she is making an effort to conceal the fact that Mary's description of the life at school has shocked her.)* Well, now I think we've had enough gossip. Dinner's almost ready.

MARY. *(Rises, crosses below Mrs. Tilford to her L. Turns to her. Softly.)* I've heard other things, too. You've always said I should tell you things that worried me.—Plenty of things I've heard worry me, Grandma.

MRS. TILFORD. What things?

MARY. Bad things.

MRS. TILFORD. Well, what were they?

MARY. I can't tell you.

MRS. TILFORD. Mary, you're annoying me very much. If you have anything to say, then say it and stop acting silly.

MARY. I mean I can't say it out loud.

MRS. TILFORD. There couldn't possibly be anything you couldn't say out loud. Now either tell me what's worrying you, or be still.

MARY. Well, a lot of things I don't understand. But it's awful, and sometimes they fight and then they make up, and Miss Dobie cries and Miss Wright gets mad, and then they make up again, and there are funny noises and we get scared.

MRS. TILFORD. Noises? I suppose you girls have a happy time imagining a murder.

MARY. And we've seen things, too. Funny things. *(Sees the impatience of Mrs. Tilford.)* I'd tell you, but I got to whisper it.

MRS. TILFORD. Why must you whisper it?

MARY. I don't know. I just got to. *(Leans over back of Mrs. Tilford's chair and begins whispering. At first the whisper is slow and hesitant, but it gradually works itself up to fast, excited talking. In the middle of it, Mrs. Tilford stops her.)*

MRS. TILFORD. *(Trembling.)* What are you saying? *(Without answering Mary goes back to the whispering until the older woman takes her by the shoulders and turns her around to stare in her face.)* I don't believe you know what you're saying, Mary! *Are you telling me the truth?* (Mary whispers again briefly. After a moment Mrs. Tilford gets up, moves away R. She is no longer listening to Mary, who keeps up a running fire of conversation.)*

MARY. Honest, honest. You just ask Peggy and Evelyn and—They know, too. Just get them here and ask them. And maybe there're other kids who know, but we've always been frightened and so we didn't ask, and one night I was going to go and find out, but I got scared and we went to bed early so we wouldn't hear, but sometimes I couldn't help it, but we never talked about it much, because we thought they'd find out and. It's in a lot of books—I mean—One of the girls at camp—I mean—Oh, Grandma, don't make me go back to that awful place!

MRS. TILFORD. *(Abstractedly.)* What?

MARY. *(Moves toward Mrs. Tilford.)* Don't make me go back to that place. I just couldn't stand it anymore. Really, Grandma, I'm so unhappy there, and if only I could stay out the rest of the term, why, then—*I* don't understand, but—

MRS. TILFORD. *(Makes irritated gesture.)* Be still a minute. *(After a moment, turns to Mary.)* Have you told me the truth?

MARY. I swear on the grave of my father. Please don't send me back—

MRS. TILFORD. *(Looks at her.)* No, you won't have to go back.

MARY. *(Surprised.)* Honest? Oh! Oh, you're the nicest, loveliest grandma in all the world. You—you're not mad at me?

MRS. TILFORD. I'm not mad at you. Now go upstairs. *(Mary walks slowly up to arch. She pauses there for a moment, looks back at her grandmother, then goes off R. Mrs. Tilford stands for a long moment, then very slowly walks up to arch, pauses, crosses to phone. Dials a number.)* Is Miss Wright—is Miss Wright in? *(Waits a second, hurriedly puts down receiver.)* Never mind, never mind. *(Thinks for a moment, then dials another number.)* Dr. Cardin, please. Mrs. Tilford. *(She remains absolutely motionless while she waits. When she does speak, her voice is low and tense.)* Joseph? Joseph? Can you come to see me right away? Yes, I'm perfectly well. No, but it's important, Joseph, very important. I must see you right away. I—I can't tell you over the phone. Can't you come sooner? It's not about Mary's fainting—I said it's not about Mary, Joseph; in one way it's about Mary— *(Suddenly quiet.)* But will the hospital take so long? Very well, Joseph, make it as soon as you can. *(Hangs up receiver, sits in chair R. of console table and for a moment is undecided. Then, taking a breath, she dials another number.)* Mrs. Munn, please. This is Mrs. Tilford. Miriam? This is Amelia Tilford. Miriam, I need to see you immediately. No, I am sorry to interrupt, but it must be now. Miriam! It has to do with the school—something very shocking, I am afraid—something that has to do with Evelyn and Mary—Yes, immediately, please— *(She rises, slowly exits through arch. Going off R. as the CURTAIN FALLS.)*

40

Scene 2

SCENE: *The same as Scene 1. The curtain has been lowered to mark the passing of a few hours.*

AT RISE: *Mary is lying on the floor downstage of R. love seat, playing with a jigsaw puzzle, and singing, "Oh Dear What Can the Matter Be." Agatha appears from D. L., lugging blankets and pillows across the room. She stops L. of L. loveseat and gives Mary an annoyed look.*

AGATHA. And see to it that she doesn't get the good blankets all dirty, and let her wear your green pyjamas.

MARY. Who?

AGATHA. Who? Don't you ever keep your ears open? Rosalie Wells is coming over to spend the night with you.

MARY. *(Sits up.)* You mean she's going to sleep *here*?

AGATHA. You heard me.

MARY. What for?

AGATHA. Do I know all the crazy things that are happening around here? Your grandmother phoned Mrs. Wells all the way to New York, five dollars and eighty-five cents thrown out, and Mrs. Wells wanted to know if Rosalie could stay here until tomorrow.

MARY. *(Relieved.)* Oh. Couldn't Evelyn Munn come instead?

AGATHA. Sure. We'll have the whole town over to entertain you.

MARY. I won't let Rosalie Wells wear my new pyjamas. *(Front doorbell rings.)*

AGATHA. *(Exits through, goes off L.)* Don't tell me what you won't do. You'll act like a lady for once in your life. *(Offstage.)* Come on in, Rosalie. Just go on in there and make yourself at home. Have you had your dinner?

ROSALIE. *(Enters, stands L. of arch.)* Good evening. Yes'm.

AGATHA. *(Who has followed her in.)* Take off your pretty coat. Have you had your bath?

ROSALIE. *(Taking off coat.)* Yes, ma'am. This morning.

AGATHA. Well, you better have another one. *(She takes Rosalie's coat and exits through arch, goes off R. Mary, lying in front of love seat, is hidden from her. Gingerly, Rosalie sits down on chair L. of arch.)*

MARY. *(Loudly.)* Whooooo! *(Rosalie jumps up.)* Whooooo! *(Rosalie, frightened, starts hurriedly for door. Mary sits up, laughs.)* You're a goose.

ROSALIE. *(Comes down to below L. end of L. love seat. Belligerently.)* Oh, so it's you. Well, who likes to hear funny noises at night? You could have been a werewolf.

MARY. What would a werewolf do with you?

ROSALIE. *(Crossing R. to armchair.)* Just what he'd do with anybody else. *(Mary laughs.)* Isn't it funny about school?

MARY. What's funny about it?

ROSALIE. *(Crosses upstage, inspects sideboard.)* Don't act like you can come home every night.

MARY. Maybe I can from now on. *(Rolls over on her back luxuriously.)* Maybe I'm never going back.

ROSALIE. Am I going back? I don't want to stay home.

MARY. What'll you give to know?

ROSALIE. *(Takes a grape.)* Nothing. I'll just ask my mother.

MARY. Will you give me a free T.L. if I tell you?

ROSALIE. *(Comes to behind R. of love seat. Thinks for a moment.)* All right. Lois Fisher told Helen that you were very smart.

MARY. That's an old one. I won't take it.

ROSALIE. You got to take it.

MARY. Nope.

ROSALIE. *(Laughs.)* You don't know anyway.

MARY. I know what I heard, and I know Grandma phoned your mother in New York five dollars and eighty-five cents to come and get you right away. You're just going to spend the night here. I wish Evelyn could come instead of you.

ROSALIE. *(Comes down to R. of R. love seat.)* But what's happened? Peggy and Helen and Evelyn and Lois went home tonight, too. Do you think somebody's got secret measles or something?

MARY. No.

ROSALIE. Do *you* know what it is? How'd you find out? *(No answer.)* You're always pretending you know everything. You're just faking. *(Flounces away. Sits on ottoman.)* Never mind, don't bother telling me. I think curiosity is very unladylike, anyhow. I have no concern with your silly secrets, none at all. *(She twirls round on ottoman, stops and after long pause.)* What did you say?

MARY. I didn't say a thing.

ROSALIE. Oh. *(Twirls around again.)*

MARY. *(Laughs. Rises, puts jigsaw puzzle in a drawer of highboy.)* But now suppose I told you that I just may have said that you were in on it?

ROSALIE. *(Stops twirling.)* In on what?

MARY. *(Comes down to R. of R. love seat.)* The secret. Suppose I told you that I *may have* said that you told me about it?

ROSALIE. *(Rises.)* Why, Mary Tilford! You can't do a thing like that. I didn't tell you about anything. *(Mary laughs.)* Did you tell your grandmother such a thing?

MARY. Maybe.

ROSALIE. *(Crosses to below R. love seat, turns to Mary.)* Well, I'm going right up to your grandmother and tell I didn't tell you anything—whatever it is. You're just trying to get me into trouble, like always, and I'm not going to let you. *(Starts for arch.)*

MARY. *(Crosses to below armchair.)* Wait a minute, I'll come with you.

ROSALIE. *(Stops U. L. of armchair.)* What for?

MARY. I want to tell her about Helen Burton's bracelet.

ROSALIE. *(Slowly turns to Mary.)* What about it?

MARY. Just that you stole it.

ROSALIE. *(Crosses to Mary.)* Shut up! I didn't do any such thing.

MARY. Yes, you did.

ROSALIE. *(Tearfully.)* You made it up. You're always making things up.

MARY. You can't call me a liar, Rosalie Wells. That's a kind of dare and I won't take a dare. *(She starts for arch. Rosalie blocks her way.)* I guess I'll go tell Grandma, anyway. Then she can call the police and they'll come for you and, you'll get tried in court. *(She slowly backs Rosalie to behind R. end of L. love seat. While she speaks, she pulls Rosalie's glasses down on her nose and pulls her hair.)* And you'll go to one of those prisons, and you'll get older and older, and when you're good and old they'll let you out, but your mother and father will be dead by then and you won't have any place to go and you'll beg on the streets—

ROSALIE. *(Crying.)* I didn't steal anything. I borrowed the bracelet and I was going to put it back as soon as I'd worn it to the movies. I never meant to keep it.

MARY. Nobody'll believe that, least of all the police. You're just a common, ordinary thief. Stop that bawling. You'll have the whole house down here in a minute.

ROSALIE. You won't tell? Say you won't tell.

MARY. Am I a liar?

ROSALIE. No.

MARY. Then say: "I apologize on my hands and knees."

ROSALIE. I apologize on my hands and knees. Let's play with the puzzle.

MARY. Wait a minute. Say: "From now on, I, Rosalie Wells— *(Crosses her wrists in front of her.)* am the vassal of Mary Tilford and will do and say whatever she tells me under the solemn oath of a knight."

ROSALIE. *(Crosses downstage to below R. end of love seat.)* I won't say that. That's the worst oath there is. *(Mary starts down R.)* Mary! Please don't— *(She quickly follows Mary and stops her below R. love seat.)*

MARY. Will you swear it?

ROSALIE. *(Sniffling.)* But then you could tell me to do anything.

MARY. *(Starts to move R.)* Say it quick or I'll—

ROSALIE. *(Hurriedly.)* From now on— *(Slowly turns and crosses L. to L. love seat, holding her wrists crossed in front of her.)* I, Rosalie Wells, am the vassal of Mary Tilford and will do and say whatever she tells me under the solemn oath of a knight.

MARY. Don't forget that.

MRS. TILFORD. *(Enters from D. R., crosses to Rosalie.)* Good evening, Rosalie, you're looking very well.

ROSALIE. Good evening, Mrs. Tilford.

MARY. She's getting fatter every day.

MRS. TILFORD. *(Abstractedly.)* Then it's very becoming. *(Doorbell rings.)* That must be Joseph. Mary, take Rosalie into the library. There's some fruit and milk on the table. Be sure you're both fast asleep by half-past ten. *(Rosalie starts to exit R., sees Mary, stops, hesitates.)*

MARY. Go on, Rosalie. *(She pushes Rosalie, waits until she reluctantly exits D. R.)* Grandma.

MRS. TILFORD. Yes?

MARY. *(Crosses to her.)* Grandma, Cousin Joe'll say I've got to go back. He'll say I really wasn't— *(Cardin enters and she runs off D. R.)*

CARDIN. Hello, Amelia. *(Looks curiously at the fleeing Mary.)*

MRS. TILFORD. Hello, Joseph. How are you?

CARDIN. Mary home?

MRS. TILFORD. *(Crosses up L. of armchair to sideboard.)* Whisky?

CARDIN. Please. *(Her hands are shaking and she spills drink. He goes to sideboard, takes it from her, pours himself a drink.)* Headaches again?

MRS. TILFORD. No.

CARDIN. What's the matter with your hands?

MRS. TILFORD. *(Crosses D. C., sits in armchair.)* Nothing. How have you been, Joseph?

CARDIN. Fine.

MRS. TILFORD. *(Vaguely, sparring for time.)* I haven't seen you the last few weeks. Agatha misses you for Sunday dinners.

CARDIN. *(Crosses D. R. Sits on L. end of R. love seat.)* I've been busy. We're getting the results from the mating season right about now.

MRS. TILFORD. Did I take you away from a patient?

CARDIN. No. I was at the hospital. I told you that.

MRS. TILFORD. How is the hospital? How's it getting on?

CARDIN. Just the same. Not enough money, badly equipped, everybody growling at everybody else—Amelia, you didn't bring me here to talk about the hospital. What's the matter with you?

MRS. TILFORD. I—I have something to tell you.

CARDIN. Well, out with it. *(Pause.)* Yes?

MRS. TILFORD. It's a very hard thing to say, Joseph.

CARDIN. Hard for you to say to me? *(No answer.)* Don't be worried about Mary. I guessed that she ran home to tell you about her faint. It was caused by nothing but bad temper and was clumsily managed, at that. Amelia, she's a terribly spoilt—

MRS. TILFORD. I heard about the faint. That's not what is worrying me.

CARDIN. You're in trouble, Amelia?

MRS. TILFORD. Yes. We all are in trouble. Bad trouble.

CARDIN. We? Me, you mean? Nothing's the matter with me.

MRS. TILFORD. When did you last see Karen?

CARDIN. Today. This afternoon.

MRS. TILFORD. Oh. Not since seven o'clock?

CARDIN. What's happened since seven o'clock?

MRS. TILFORD. Joseph, you've been engaged to Karen for a long time. Are your plans any more definite than they were a year ago?

CARDIN. You can buy the wedding present. And we'll be married in this room, the way you and I planned it long before we knew the girl—

MRS. TILFORD. Why has Karen suddenly decided to make it definite?

CARDIN. It's always been definite. You know very well that up to the last year I've been paying back the money I borrowed for medical school and—You know all that. Now I'm all right, and the school is pretty well on its feet. There's even enough money to support Mrs. Mortar some other place and so Martha will be better off and—

MRS. TILFORD. I've already heard that they were putting Mrs. Mortar out.

CARDIN. Putting her out? It's about time. But the promise that a good niece will support you for the rest of your life is a mighty nice way of being put out.

MRS. TILFORD. You don't—Don't you find it odd that they want so much to get rid of that silly woman? She's harmless enough—

CARDIN. *(Smiles.)* You don't know what you're talking about, Amelia. You've never been around her. Lily Mortar is not a harmless woman, although God knows she's silly enough. She's a nasty, tiresome, spoilt old bitch and if you're feeling sorry for her you're wasting your time. *(Mrs. Tilford rises, moves L.)* Now it's not like you to waste your time. Or to waste mine. What did you call me here for?

MRS. TILFORD. *(Turns to Cardin.)* You must not marry Karen.

CARDIN. *(Shocked, grins.)* Why must I not marry Karen? *(Then very sharply, rises, putting drink on table.)* What are you talking about? Why must I not marry Karen?

MRS. TILFORD. Because there's something wrong with Karen— something horrible. *(Doorbell rings, loud, long.)*

CARDIN. *(Slowly, coldly.)* And there is something very wrong with you for thinking you can talk this way to me.

MRS. TILFORD. I know what I am talking about—

KAREN. *(Off.)* Mrs. Tilford, Agatha. Is she in?

MRS. TILFORD. *(Breaks off as she hears voices offstage.)* Who is that?

AGATHA. *(Off.)* Yes'm. Come on in.

MRS. TILFORD. I won't have her here.

CARDIN. *(Angrily.)* What are you talking about?

MRS. TILFORD. *(Crosses in front of Cardin to below R. end of love seat.)* I won't have her here.

CARDIN. Then you don't want me here, either. *(Moves to Karen, who, with Martha, has rushed in. He meets Karen L. of armchair. Martha crosses R. to above love seat.)* Darling, what is all this? What?

KAREN. What happened, Joe? Is it a joke, Joe?

MARTHA. *(With great force to Mrs. Tilford.)* We've come to find out what you are doing.

CARDIN. What is it?

46

KAREN. I don't know. I don't know. What did she do it for?

CARDIN. What are you talking about? What do you mean?

MRS. TILFORD. *(Below R. end of R. love seat.)* You shouldn't have come here.

CARDIN. What is all this? What's happened?

KAREN. I tried to reach you. I tried and tried. Hasn't she told you?

CARDIN. Nobody's told me anything. I haven't heard anything but wild talk. What is it, Karen? *(She starts to speak, then dumbly shakes head.)* What's happened, Martha?

MARTHA. *(Violently.)* An insane asylum has been let loose. How do we know what's happened?

CARDIN. What was it?

KAREN. We didn't know what it was. Nobody would talk to us, nobody would tell us anything.

CARDIN. *(With anger.)* Stop it. Tell me what's happened.

MARTHA. *(Moves to above L. end of love seat.)* See if you can make any sense out of it. At dinner-time Mrs. Munn's chauffeur arrived and said that Evelyn must be sent home right away. At half-past seven Mrs. Burton came to tell us that she wanted Helen's things packed immediately and that she'd wait outside because she didn't want to enter a place like ours. Five minutes later the Wells's butler came for Rosalie.

CARDIN. Why? Why?

MARTHA. It was a madhouse. People rushing in and out, the children being pushed into cars, Karen and I begging people to tell us, nobody answering us—

KAREN. *(Quiet now, takes his hand.)* Mrs. Rogers finally told us.

CARDIN. What?

KAREN. That—that Martha and I have been—have been lovers. Mrs. Tilford told them.

CARDIN. *(For a moment stands staring at her incredulously. Then finally turns to Mrs. Tilford, stares at her a moment.)* Did you tell them that?

MRS. TILFORD. Yes.

CARDIN. Are you sick? Are you a sick woman?

MRS. TILFORD. You know I'm not sick.

CARDIN. *(Snapping the words out.)* Then what did you do it for?

MRS. TILFORD. *(Slowly.)* Because it's true.

KAREN. *(Incredulously. Crosses to below R. love seat.)* You think it's true, then?

MARTHA. You crazy, crazy, crazy, old woman!

KAREN. You mean you did say it? You knew what you were saying? You—

MRS. TILFORD. *(Crosses to Karen.)* Yes. I knew what I was saying. I don't think you should have come here.

MARTHA. *(Crossing L. to above L. love seat.)* You damned, vicious—

MRS. TILFORD. *(Crosses to Martha. Quietly.)* I shall not call you names, and I will not allow you to call me names. You should not have come here. I don't trust myself to talk about it with you now or ever.

KAREN. What's she talking about, Joe? What's she mean? What is she trying to do to us? What did she do it for? *(Cardin goes to Karen and puts his arms around her.)*

MARTHA. *(Softly, as though to herself.)* We're being pushed around by a crazy woman. *(Shakes herself slightly.)* That's an awful thing. And we're standing here—We're standing here taking it. Didn't you know we'd come here? *(Suddenly, with violence.)* Were we supposed to lie down and smile while you took up a gun and looked around for people to kill?

MRS. TILFORD. This can't do any of us any good, Miss Dobie.

MARTHA. "This can't do any of us any good." Listen, listen! You're not playing with paper dolls. We're human beings, see? We're people. It's our lives you're playing with. *Our* lives. That's serious business for us. Can you understand that?

MRS. TILFORD. *(For the first time she speaks angrily.)* I can understand that, and I understand a lot more. *You've* been playing with a lot of children's lives; and that's why I stopped you. *(More calmly.)* I know how serious this is for you, how serious it is for all of us.

CARDIN. *(Bitterly.)* I don't think you do know. I don't think so. *(Cardin crosses R. below Karen to R. end of love seat.)*

MRS. TILFORD. I wanted to avoid this meeting because it can't do any good. You came here to find out if I had made the charge. You've found out. Let's end it there. *I don't want you in this house.* *(Turns to Cardin.)* I'm sorry this had to be done to you, Joseph.

CARDIN. Don't talk to me like that, Amelia, *please.*

MRS. TILFORD. *(Comes D. C.)* Very well. There's nothing I mean to do, nothing I want to do. There's nothing anybody can do.

CARDIN. *(Carefully.)* You have done a terrible thing.

MRS. TILFORD. I have done what I had to do. What they are may possibly be their own business. It becomes a great deal more than that when children are concerned in it. Children—

KAREN. *(Wildly.)* It's not true! Not a word of it is true; can't you understand that? *(Cardin sits on R. end of love seat.)*

MRS. TILFORD. There won't be any punishment for either of you. But there mustn't be any punishment for me, either—and that's what this meeting is. *(Moves L., sits in L. end of L. love seat.)* This—this thing is your own. Go away with it. I don't understand it and I don't want any part of it. Take it out of here.

MARTHA. *(Slowly.)* So you think we should go away?

MRS. TILFORD. I think that's best for you.

MARTHA. *(Moves upstage.)* There must be something we can do to you, and, whatever it is, we must find it.

MRS. TILFORD. That will be very unwise.

CARDIN. Do you know what's wise? *(Violently.)* You are an irresponsible old woman, that's all—

KAREN. *(Crosses to R. of L. love seat.)* It makes me dirty and sick to stand here and defend myself—and against what? Against a lie. A great, awful lie.

MRS. TILFORD. I'm sorry that I can't believe that.

KAREN. There isn't a single word of truth in anything you said. *(Waits, then.)* Damn you. *(Karen crosses U. R. to sideboard.)*

CARDIN. They've worked eight long years to save enough money to buy that farm, to start that school. They did without everything that young people ought to have. You wouldn't know about that. That school meant things to them: self-respect, and bread and butter, and honest work. Do you know what it is to try so hard for anything? Well, now it's gone. What the hell did you do it for?

MRS. TILFORD. *(Softly. Rises.)* It had to be done.

CARDIN. *(Rises.)* Righteousness is a great thing.

MRS. TILFORD. *(Gently.)* I know how you must feel about me.

CARDIN. You don't know anything about how I feel.

MRS. TILFORD. *(Crosses to C.)* I've loved you as much as I loved my own boys. I wouldn't have spared them; I couldn't spare you.

CARDIN. *(Fiercely.)* I believe you. *(Moves away U. R.)*

MARTHA. What is there to do to you? What can we do to you? There must be something—something that makes you feel the way we do tonight. *(Comes down to L. of Mrs. Tilford.)* You don't want any part of this, you said. But you'll get a part. More than you bargained for. *(Suddenly.)* Are you willing to stand by everything you've said tonight? *(Karen comes down to above armchair.)*

MRS. TILFORD. Yes.

MARTHA. All right. That's fine. But don't get the idea we'll let you whisper this lie: you made it and you'll come out with it. Shriek it to your town of Lancet. We'll *make* you shriek it—and we'll make you do it in a court room. Tomorrow, Mrs. Tilford, you will have a libel suit on your hands.

MRS. TILFORD. *(Turns to Martha.)* Miss Dobie, don't do that.

KAREN. It's your turn to be frightened.

MRS. TILFORD. It is you I am thinking of. I am frightened for you. It was wrong of you to brazen it out here tonight; it would be criminally foolish of you to brazen it out in public. That can bring you nothing but pain. I am an old woman, Miss Dobie, and I have seen too many people act in pride and anger. In the end they punish themselves.

MARTHA. *(With great anger.)* We'll take our own way.

CARDIN. *(Comes down to R. at R. love seat.)* So you took a child's word for it?

MARTHA. *(Looks at him, shakes head.)* Yes. That's what she did.

KAREN. That is really where you got it? I can't believe—it couldn't be. Why, she's a child.

MARTHA. She's not a child.

KAREN. Oh, my God, it all fits so well now. That girl has hated us for a long time. We never knew why, we never could find out. There didn't seem to be any reason—

MARTHA. There wasn't any reason. She hates everybody and everything.

KAREN. Your Mary's a strange girl. A dark girl. There's something very awful the matter with her.

MRS. TILFORD. *(Crosses to below R. love seat.)* I was waiting for you to say that, Mss Wright.

KAREN. *(Crosses D. R., goes to Mrs. Tilford.)* I'm telling you the truth. We should have told it to you long ago. *(Stops, crosses to Martha.)* It's no use.

CARDIN. Where is she?

MRS. TILFORD. You cannot see her.

CARDIN. Where is she?

MRS. TILFORD. I won't have that, Joseph.

CARDIN. I'm going to talk to her.

MRS. TILFORD. *I won't have her go through with that again. (To Karen and Martha.)* You came here demanding explanations. It was I who should have asked them from you. You attack me, you attack

Mary. I've told you I didn't mean you any harm. I still don't. You claim that it isn't true; it may be natural that you should say that, but I *know* that it is true. No matter what you say, you know very well that I wouldn't have acted until I was sure. All I wanted was to get those children away. That has been done. There will be nothing else. And there won't be any talk about it or about you—I'll see to that. You have been in my house long enough. Get out.

KAREN. Let's go home. *(Starts to go, Martha stops her.)*

CARDIN. I want to see Mary. I'm going to see her, and you know I am not going to leave this house until I do. I've been your friend. You owe me something. Where is she? *(After a moment Mrs. Tilford motions R. Quickly Cardin goes to D. R. entrance.)* Mary! Come here. *(Mrs. Tilford moves to R. of R. love seat. After a moment Mary appears. Her manner is shy and afraid.)*

MRS. TILFORD. *(Gently.)* Sit down, dear, and don't be afraid. *(She motions to armchair. Mary slowly crosses and sits.)*

CARDIN. *(Slowly crosses and sits on L. end of R. love seat.)* Everybody lies all the time. Sometimes they have to, sometimes they don't. I've lied myself for a lot of different reasons, but there was never a time when, if I'd been given a second chance, I wouldn't have taken back the lie and told the truth. You're lucky if you ever get that chance. I'm telling you this because I'm about to ask you a question. Before you answer the question, I want to tell you that if you've l—, if you made a mistake, you must take this chance and say so. You won't be punished for it. Do you get all that?

MARY. *(Timidly.)* Yes, Cousin Joe.

CARDIN. *(Grimly.)* All right. Were you telling your grandmother the truth this afternoon? The exact truth about Miss Wright and Miss Dobie?

MARY. *(Without hesitation.)* Oh, yes. *(Karen sighs deeply, moves up to sideboard. Martha, her fists closed tight, turns her back to Mary.)*

CARDIN. All right, Mary, that was your chance; you passed it up. Now let's find out things.

MRS. TILFORD. She's told you, Joseph. That will be all. I—

CARDIN. No! No! Will you answer some more questions, Mary?

MARY. Yes, Cousin Joe.

MARTHA. Stop that sick, sweet tone of voice.

CARDIN. Why don't you like Miss Dobie and Miss Wright?

MARY. Oh, I do like them. They just don't like me, They never have liked me.

CARDIN. How do you know?

MARY. They're always picking on me. They're always punishing me for everything that happens. No matter what happens, it's always me.

CARDIN. Why do you think they do that?

MARY. Because—because they're—because they— *(Stops, looks at Mrs. Tilford.)* Grandma, I—

CARDIN. All right, all right. Did you get punished today?

MARY. Yes, and it was just because Peggy and Evelyn heard them and so they took it out on me.

KAREN. That's a lie.

CARDIN. Sssh. Heard what, Mary?

MARY. Mrs. Mortar told Miss Dobie that there was something funny about her: She said that she had a funny feeling about Miss Wright, and Mrs. Mortar said that was unnatural. That was why we got punished, just because—

KAREN. That was not the reason they got punished.

MARTHA. *(Moves to C.)* My aunt is a stupid woman. What she said was unpleasant; it was said to annoy me. It meant nothing more than that.

MARY. And, Cousin Joe, she said that every time you came to the school Miss Dobie got jealous, and that she didn't want you to get married.

MARTHA. *(To Cardin.)* She said that, too. This—this child is taking little things, little family things, and making them have meanings that— *(Stops, suddenly regards Mary with a combination of disgust and interest.)* Where did you learn so much in so little time? *(Moves away L. above love seat.)*

CARDIN. What do you think Mrs. Mortar meant by all that talk, Mary?

MRS. TILFORD. Stop it, Joseph!

MARY. I don't know, but it was always kind of funny and she always said things like that and all the girls would talk about it when Miss Dobie went and visited Miss Wright late at night—

KAREN. *(Angrily. Comes down to above R. love seat, leans over it to Mrs. Tilford.)* And we work at night and sometimes we go to the movies at night, and sometimes we read at night, and sometimes we drink tea at night. We are guilty of all those things, Mrs. Tilford.

MARY. And there are always funny sounds, and we'd stay awake and listen because we couldn't help hearing and I'd get frightened because the sounds were like—

52

MARTHA. *(Crosses to C.)* Be still!

KAREN. *(Crosses to U. R. of Mary. With violence.)* No, no. You don't want her still now. The sounds were like what?

MARY. Grandma, I—

MRS. TILFORD. *(Bitterly, to Cardin.)* Leave the child alone. It doesn't need a name. Stop—

CARDIN. *(Ignoring her—speaks to Mary.)* Go on.

MARY. I don't know; there were just sounds.

CARDIN. But what did you think they were? Why did they frighten you?

MARY. *(Weakly.)* I don't know.

CARDIN. *(Smiles at Mrs. Tilford.)* She doesn't know.

MARY. *(Nastily.)* But I saw things, too. One night there was so much noise I thought somebody was sick or something and I looked through the keyhole and they were kissing and saying things and then I got scared because it was different sort of and I—

MARTHA. *(Her face distorted, moves to U. L. of Mary. To Mrs. Tilford.)* That child—that child is sick.

KAREN. Ask her again how she could see us?

CARDIN. How could you see Miss Dobie and Miss Wright?

MARY. I—I—

MRS. TILFORD. Tell him what you whispered to me.

MARY. It was at night and I was leaning down by the keyhole. And—

KAREN. *There's no keyhole on my door.*

MRS. TILFORD. What?

KAREN. There—is—no—keyhole—on—my—door.

MARY. *(Quickly.)* It wasn't her room, Grandma, it was the other room, I guess. It was *Miss Dobie's* room. I saw them through the keyhole in Miss Dobie's room.

CARDIN. How did you know anybody was in Miss Dobie's room?

MARY. I told you, I told you. Because we heard them. Everybody heard them—

MARTHA. I share a room with my aunt. It is on the first floor at the back of the house. Mary's room is at the front of the house, at the other end. It is impossible to hear anything from there. *(To Cardin.)* Tell her to come and see for herself.

MRS. TILFORD. *(Her voice shaken. Moves toward Mary.)* What is this, Mary? Why did you say you saw through a keyhole? *Can* you hear from your room?

53

MARY. *(Starts to cry.)* Everybody is yelling at me. I don't know what I'm saying with everybody mixing me all up. I did see it! I did see it!

MRS. TILFORD. *What* did you see? *Where* did you see it? I want the truth, now. The truth, whatever it is.

CARDIN. *(Rises, crosses up to desk.)* We can go home. We are finished here. *(Looks around.)* It's an ugly house.

MRS. TILFORD. *(Angrily.)* Stop that crying, Mary. Stand up. *(Mary gets up, head down, still crying hysterically. Mrs. Tilford crosses to her.)* I want the truth.

MARY. All—all right.

MRS. TILFORD. What is the truth?

MARY. *(Pointing R.)* It was Rosalie who saw them. I just said it was me so I wouldn't have to tattle on Rosalie.

CARDIN. *(Moves L. Wearily.)* Oh, my God!

MARY. It was Rosalie, Grandma, she told us all about it. She said she had read about it in a book and she knew everything— *(Desperately.)* You ask Rosalie. You just ask Rosalie. She'll tell you. We used to talk about it all the time. That's the truth. That's the honest truth. She said it was when the door was open once and she told us all about it. I was just trying to save Rosalie, and everybody jumps on me.

MRS. TILFORD. *(To Cardin.)* Please wait a minute. *(Goes to D. R. entrance.)* Rosalie! *(Karen moves down to R. of L. love seat.)*

CARDIN. Amelia, you deserve whatever you get.

MRS. TILFORD. *(Stands waiting for Rosalie, passes hand over her face.)* I don't know. I don't know, anymore. Maybe it's what I do deserve. *(As Rosalie, frightened, appears, she takes the child gently by the hand, brings her to below L. end of L. love seat, talking nervously.)* I'm sorry to keep you up so late, Rosalie. You must be tired. *(Speaks rapidly.)* Mary says there's been a lot of talk in the school lately about Miss Wright and Miss Dobie. Is that true?

ROSALIE. I—I don't know what you mean?

MRS. TILFORD. That things have been said among the girls.

ROSALIE. *(Wide-eyed, frightened.)* What things? I never—I—I—

MRS. TILFORD. What was the talk about, Rosalie?

KAREN. *(Gently.)* Don't be frightened.

ROSALIE. *(Utterly bewildered. Goes to Karen.)* I don't know what she means, Miss Wright.

KAREN. *(Sits R. end of love seat, holds her hand out to Rosalie, who sits beside her.)* Rosalie, Mary has told her grandmother that certain things at school have been—er—puzzling you girls. You, particularly.

ROSALIE. A lot of things puzzle me. I guess I'm not very good at algebra, and Helen helps me sometimes, if that—

KAREN. No, that's not what she meant. She says that you told her that you saw certain—certain acts between Miss Dobie and myself. She says that once, when the door was open, you saw us kissing each other in a way that— *(Unable to bear Rosalie's look, she turns away.)* women don't kiss one another.

ROSALIE. Oh, Miss Wright, I didn't, didn't, I didn't. I never said such a thing.

MRS. TILFORD. *(L. of love seat. Grimly.)* That's true, my dear?

ROSALIE. I never saw any such thing. Mary always makes things up about me and everybody else. Everybody in school knows that. *(Starts to weep in excitement.)* I never said any such thing ever. Why, I never even could have thought of—

MARY. *(Staring at her, speaks very slowly. Crosses L. below Rosalie, holding her wrists crossed in front of her.)* Yes, you did, Rosalie. You're just trying to get out of it. I remember just when you said it. I remember it, because it was the day Helen Burton's bracelet was—

ROSALIE. *(Starts to rise, fascinated and fearful, looking at Mary.)* I never did. I—I—you're just—

MARY. It was the day Helen's bracelet was stolen, and nobody knew who did it, and Helen said that if her mother found out, she'd have the thief put in jail right away.

KAREN. *(Puzzled, as are the others, by sudden change in Rosalie's manner.)* There's nothing to cry about. You must help us by telling the truth. Why, what's the matter, Rosalie? *(Martha and Cardin come to behind love seat.)*

MARY. Grandma, there's something I've got to tell you that—

ROSALIE. *(With a shrill cry.)* Yes! Yes! I did see it. I told Mary. What Mary said was right. I said it, I said it, I said it— *(Throws herself on L. end of love seat, weeping hysterically, Martha, Karen, Cardin, and Mrs. Tilford are staring at Rosalie: Mary slowly smiles as the...)*

CURTAIN FALLS

ACT III

SCENE: *The same as Act I. Living rooms of the school.*

AT RISE: *The room has changed. It is not actually dirty, but it is dull and dark and uncared for. The windows are lightly shut, curtains tightly drawn. Karen is sitting in chair, U. L. of D. R. table, feet flat on the floor. She is holding a book in her lap. Martha, holding a cup of coffee, is pacing about the room. As curtain rises, she is above desk, moving R. She crosses to above sofa, turns, comes downstage, L. of sofa, and crosses to stove.*

MARTHA. *(In front of stove.)* It's cold in here.
KAREN. Yes.
MARTHA. *(Crossing upstage L. above desk.)* What time is it?
KAREN. I don't know. What's the difference?
MARTHA. None. I was hoping it was time for my bath. *(Puts cup down on saucer, which is on desk.)*
KAREN. Take it early today.
MARTHA. *(Laughs. Crosses R. above sofa.)* Oh, I couldn't do that. I look forward all day to that bath. Makes me feel important to know there's one thing I've got to do. *(Turns, comes downstage, left of sofa, crosses to below desk.)* Six o'clock take a bath, like you've always done. You know yesterday, I took a six o'clock bath and I took another at four this morning. *(Turns to Karen.)* Your light was on. I wanted to bring you some milk but I just went back to bed and—I'm going to do it again tonight. *(Crosses to stove.)* I'm going to have a four o'clock bath and watch the light come up. And I'm going to wash my hair tonight, or maybe tomorrow night. Why don't you do that? Gives you something to do, a kind of date with something—
KAREN. It's raining. Hungry?
MARTHA. No. *(Phone rings. Neither of them pays the slightest attention to it, until the ringing becomes too insistent. Then Martha crosses to it, takes receiver off, crosses to below sofa. Lies down facing Karen.)*

KAREN. You must eat something tonight.

MARTHA. I'd like to be hungry again. Remember how much we used to eat at college? All that wonderful mess every evening—

KAREN. That was ten years ago. *(Smiles.)* We've gotten older. You must try to eat dinner tonight.

MARTHA. Maybe I'll be hungry in another ten years. It's cheaper this way.

KAREN. Joe is late today. What time is it?

MARTHA. *(Turns again to lie on her side.)* We've been sitting here for eight days asking each other the time.

KAREN. It's been eight days since we've been out of this house.

MARTHA. Well, we'll have to get off these chairs sooner or later. In a couple of months they'll need dusting.

KAREN. What'll we do when we get off?

MARTHA. Dust the chairs.

KAREN. *(Almost in a whisper.)* It's awful.

MARTHA. Let's not talk about it. *(After a moment.)* Let's eat a good dinner tonight. What about eggs for dinner?

KAREN. All right.

MARTHA. I'll make some potatoes with onions, the way you used to like them.

KAREN. It's a week ago Thursday. It never seemed real until the last day, although I guessed it before that, didn't you?

MARTHA. It seems real enough now, all right.

KAREN. *(Suddenly.)* Let's go out.

MARTHA. *(Turns over, stares at her.)* Where to?

KAREN. We'll take a walk.

MARTHA. Where'll we walk?

KAREN. Why shouldn't we take a walk? We won't see anybody, and suppose we do, what of it? We'll jus—

MARTHA. *(Slowly gets up and crosses upstage, left of sofa, toward door.)* Come on. We'll go through the park. *(Karen rises and crosses behind sofa toward door. They almost reach door when they stop, stare out the door for a moment and slowly turn back. Martha goes back, L. of sofa, and sits C. of sofa. Karen goes back R. of sofa, sits at R. end.)*

KAREN. We'll go tomorrow.

MARTHA. *(Laughs.)* No, we won't.

KAREN. But Joe says we've got to go out. He says that all the people who don't think it's true will begin to wonder if we keep hiding this way.

MARTHA. If it makes you feel better to think there *are* such people, go ahead.

KAREN. He says we must go into town and go shopping and act as though—

MARTHA. Shopping? That's a sound idea. There aren't three stores in Lancet that would sell us anything. Hasn't he heard about the ladies' clubs and their meetings and their circulars and their visits and their—?

KAREN. *(Softly.)* Don't tell him.

MARTHA. *(Gently.)* I won't. *(There are footsteps in hall.)* There's our friend. *(A grocery boy appears lugging a box. He crosses down C. and stands staring at them, examining them. They sit tense, looking away from him. Without taking his eyes from them, he speaks.)*

GROCERY BOY. I knocked on the kitchen door, but nobody answered.

MARTHA. You said that yesterday. All right. Thanks. Goodbye. *(He continues to stare.)*

KAREN. *(Unable any longer to stand the stare.)* Stop it.

GROCERY BOY. Here are the things. *(Giggles. Suddenly Martha thrusts her hand in the air.)*

MARTHA. I've got eight fingers, see? I'm a freak.

GROCERY BOY. *(Crosses to above desk, puts box on it.)* There's a car outside. Been there every time I came down the road. *(Gets no answer, starts backing out of door, still looking. Familiarly.)* Goodbye, girls! *(Exits.)*

MARTHA. *(Bitterly.)* You still think we should go into town?

KAREN. I don't know. I don't know about anything anymore. *(After a moment.)* Martha, Martha.

MARTHA. *(Gently.)* What is it, Karen?

KAREN. Why did it happen, and what happened? What are we doing here like this?

MARTHA. I don't know. It's as if we're in a nightmare. The kind you get when you feel as if you're way below the world and are struggling up and up sweating, sweating to come out in your own bed, your own room, coming up and up, and out— *(After a second.)* Only now I don't come out—

KAREN. *(Rises, moves R.)* We've got to get out of this place. We've got to get out quick.

MARTHA. You'll be getting married soon. Everything will be all right then.

58

KAREN. *(Vaguely.)* Yes.

MARTHA. *(Looks up.)* What is it?

KAREN. *(Sits in chair U. L. of D. R. table.)* Nothing.

MARTHA. *(Lies down with her head stage L.)* It'll be a good day. And a happy one for me. Maybe the happiest one of my life. What's the matter?

KAREN. Nothing, Martha.

MARTHA. There mustn't be anything wrong between you and Joe. Never, never.

KAREN. Nothing's wrong. *(Footsteps heard in hall. Her face lights up.)* There's Joe now. *(Mrs. Mortar, small suitcase in hand, stands in doorway. She smiles, timidly. Martha turns over, lies on her stomach, leans on her elbows, stares at Mrs. Mortar. Nobody speaks.)*

MARTHA. *(Turns back, puts hands over her eyes, speaks to Karen.)* Tell me, who is standing in the doorway?

KAREN. Looks like your aunt. But that's not possible, is it?

MRS. MORTAR. *(Smiling.)* Hello. *(After a second.)* Here I am. *(Nobody answers. She puts suitcase down R. of doorway, moves D.S., holding hand out to Martha.)* Can I come in? *(Martha ignores her. Mrs. Mortar sits in chair R. of desk. Martha turns on her side, stares at Mrs. Mortar.)* I am very glad to see you both. How is everything?

MARTHA. *(Too pleasant.)* Everything's fine. How are you?

MRS. MORTAR. *(Takes off her fur cape, shakes it, puts it on her lap.)* A little tired. Long train trip—

MARTHA. Of course. Is there something I can get you?

MRS. MORTAR. You know, I would like a cup of tea. But don't you bother—

MARTHA. No bother at all. China tea, English tea, a few little sandwiches? It's a cold day. Perhaps a whisky and soda?

MRS. MORTAR. Why, Martha. *(Comfortably, after a second.)* You know, I think I'll take—

MARTHA. *(Springs to her feet, crosses to L. of sofa.)* Where the hell have you been?

MRS. MORTAR. I've been on tour. You know that. Mostly one-night stands, although we played a ghastly week in Detroit, as ugly a city—But the whole theater has changed. They will not accept a serious play on the road. No question of it. Musicals, musicals, musicals.

MARTHA. *(Sits on arm of sofa.)* Isn't that interesting? Is it a trend, will it pass?

MRS. MORTAR. I don't know. I really just don't know. I was interviewed— *(She begins to look in her bag.)* in San Francisco— and I said, quite frankly, that perhaps a whole culture is changing. It's possible.

MARTHA. You think so? A whole culture! My, that would be too bad. I'll be so interested in your telling me about it.

KAREN. Don't.

MARTHA. *(To Karen.)* You see, it's this way: I'm trying to keep from killing her. *(Mrs. Mortar rises, crosses L. below desk. Martha rises. Violently.)* Why didn't you answer our telegrams? Answer me.

MRS. MORTAR. *(Turns to Martha.)* I told you I was moving around a great deal.

MARTHA. Don't tell me you didn't get them! You did.

KAREN. *(Wearily, to Martha.)* Oh, what difference does it all make now?

MRS. MORTAR. *(Quickly.)* Karen is quite right. Let bygones be bygones. *(Moves toward Martha.)* Martha, remember when you were a little girl and I used to complain there were never any nice toilets backstage. Well, you just should see now what—

MARTHA. Why did you refuse to come back here and testify for us?

MRS. MORTAR. I didn't refuse. I was on tour. That's a moral obligation. I just couldn't leave—

MARTHA. How did you get out of the summons? Did you live in the toilets?

MRS. MORTAR. *(Quickly.)* I don't think it was nice to try to bring me back that way. I just don't think it was. But we'll talk about that another day. For goodness' sakes, let's not go on this way. Words, words, words. My trunk's at the station.

KAREN. Mrs. Mortar, things have changed here.

MARTHA. *(Quietly.)* Yes, they've changed. *(To Mrs. Mortar, who backs away L.)* Listen to me tell you what you are pretending not to know: Karen Wright and Martha Dobie brought a suit for slander against a woman called Tilford—

MRS. MORTAR. *(Delighted she can interrupt.)* Oh, I meant to tell you. She's outside in a car. I saw her as I got out of my taxi. She called to me. Imagine that. She's right up the road—Imagine that, calling to me—

MARTHA. *(Moves toward Mrs. Mortar.)* Be still and listen to me. We brought a suit for slander against a woman called Tilford because her grandchild had accused us of having what the judge called "sinful sexual knowledge of one another." *(Mrs. Mortar holds up her hand in protest. Moves away L.)* A large part of Mrs. Tilford's defense was based on remarks made by Lily Mortar against her niece, Martha. And a greater part of the defense's case rested on the fact that Mrs. Mortar would not appear in court to explain or deny those remarks. Mrs. Mortar had a moral obligation to the theater. As you probably read in the newspapers, we lost the case.

MRS. MORTAR. I didn't think of it that way, Martha. It couldn't have done any good for all of us to get mixed up in that unpleasant notoriety— *(Martha turns, crosses U. C. Mrs. Mortar moves up L. of desk. Hastily.)* But now that you've explained it, why, I do see it your way, and I'm sorry I didn't come back. But now that I am here, I'm going to stand shoulder to shoulder with you. I know what you've gone through, but the body and heart do recover, you know. I'll be here right along with you and we'll—

MARTHA. *(Moves to R. of chair upstage of desk.)* There's an eight o'clock train. Get on it.

MRS. MORTAR. *(L. of chair upstage of desk.)* Martha!

MARTHA. You've come back because you had no place else to go. There's nothing here for you. All my grown life I've been something for you to pick dry. Get out and don't come back!

MRS. MORTAR. *(Sniffling a little.)* How can you talk to me like that?

MARTHA. Because I hate you. I've always hated you.

MRS. MORTAR. *(Gently.)* God will punish you for that.

MARTHA. *(Moves D. C.)* He's been doing all right.

MRS. MORTAR. *(Crosses to doorway, picks up suitcase.)* I'll wait upstairs until train time. You'll be sorry, Martha, for what you said to me. Because you have a good heart, and I know you love me and are grateful to me.

MARTHA. *(Crosses to below desk.)* Every fool in the world thinks that about everybody else. *(Mrs. Mortar is on her way out of door. She almost bumps into Cardin.)*

MRS. MORTAR. How do you do?

CARDIN. Look who's here! A couple of weeks late, aren't you?

MRS. MORTAR. So it's you. Now, I call that loyal. A lot of men wouldn't still be here. *(To Karen.)* You are a very lucky girl—

MARTHA. *(Goes to her.)* Get out of here. *(Mrs. Mortar exits, goes upstairs.)*

KAREN. *(Rises. Crosses to below R. end of sofa.)* Watch the time, Mrs. Mortar. Be sure you're on the train.

CARDIN. Why did she come back?

MARTHA. *(Crosses to below desk.)* She's broke.

CARDIN. We'll give her some money and get rid of her. *(Crosses to Martha, takes her hands, they are shaking.)* Stop it now. She isn't worth all that. Get finished with her for good. *(Martha nods, moves L. to stove. Cardin goes to Karen.)* What did you do today?

KAREN. We stayed here. We started to go out but—

CARDIN. *(Shakes his head.)* You promised me yesterday, both of you. Do you feel all right?

KAREN. *(Smiles, nods, leans over to kiss him. He puts his cigarette out, in ashtray on end table L. of sofa. She draws back.)* Why did you do that?

CARDIN. Do what?

KAREN. *(Softly.)* Draw away from me.

CARDIN. *(Sits on sofa.)* I didn't draw away from you. What kind of talk is that? I was putting out a cigarette. *(He holds his hand out to her. She ignores it.)* We sit around here much longer, we'll all be bats. And so we're not going to sit around here. I sold my place this morning to Foster.

KAREN. *(Sits beside him.)* You can't do that. You can't— *(Martha crosses to below chair L. of desk.)*

CARDIN. We're getting married this week. I'll give both of you two days to pack and close the place. On Thursday we'll be on a train—

KAREN. You can't leave here. I won't have you do this. You must go to Foster right away—You can't leave here—

CARDIN. Now don't let's have any of that talk, because it's all done and over. And last week I wrote to Jake Sundstrom. You remember, my old and good friend. I've told you about him so often— *(He is speaking fast. Now to Martha.)* We roomed together at school and at college. Then he changed his mind about medicine and went home. His family is very rich, they own half the state, I think—

KAREN. I am not going to let you leave here. I am not going to let you.

CARDIN. Well, Jake's fixed it for me. He found the right place. You know, it's farm country, mostly Swedes, and he says they need a doctor bad. It's going to be tough going at first, we'll be out in the middle of nowhere, but we'll live cheap and there'll be plenty for all of us—

MARTHA. Joe, Joe. I'm not going with you. I couldn't go with you. But I thank you from the bottom of my heart.

CARDIN. *(Rises, crosses to C.)* You're coming with us. Do you think we'd leave you? We want you to come. It's going to be good. Kind of fun to start all over again. I'm looking forward to what I can do in country like that. Good for doctors, to get out where it's hard, and to learn something

KAREN. *(Rises.)* You don't want to go.

CARDIN. *(Crosses U. L. of sofa.)* No, I don't want to go. This was my place, where I was born, where I wanted to be. You wanted to stay here, too. Well, to hell with all that. We can't stay. So we're going to a place where we can live, and where I've got a good friend who understands, and will help us. *(Goes to Karen.)* Most of the world doesn't live where it wants to live, or do what it wants to do. I'm not going to cry about us. Now don't talk about it any more. Please, darling.

KAREN. *(After a second.)* Yes. *(Crosses below Cardin to desk.)*

MARTHA. *(To Karen.)* Joe is right. But I can't go. It's better for all of us if I don't go.

CARDIN. You're coming with us. It wouldn't be happy for us if you didn't. Later on, you'll leave if you want to, and then I won't say no. All right?

MARTHA. All right. And I thank you. *(She crosses up L. of desk. Gets box of groceries.)*

CARDIN. You'll both need warm coats and boots. We'll stop in Boston for a day and buy things for you.

MARTHA. I'm going to make a good omelet now. A very good one. *(She exits L., closing door.)*

CARDIN. *(Crosses, sits in chair R. of desk.)* You'll like Jake and he'll like you. I've never seen his wife. God, the time we spent as kids talking about the women we were going to have or marry or something, and the places we were going to go together! Then I came back here and never saw him again—

KAREN. *(Leaning against front of desk.)* Yes, it was right for you to come back. You're a part of this place and a good part. You'll be coming back some day.

CARDIN. No. It isn't what I thought it was. My people— *(Laughs.)* My people aren't what I thought they were. I want no more of it.

KAREN. I've done this to you. I've taken away everything you wanted—

CARDIN. *(Holds her hand.)* And when we get there and find ourselves a place to live, we'll take a fishing trip for a honeymoon. It's beautiful country, and—

KAREN. Everything we wanted, everything we were going to be—all gone. And we have to sneak away to some place that hasn't anything to do with us—

CARDIN. *Please stop talking that way.* We've got a chance, but I think it's only one chance, and if we miss it we're done for. And that means that we are going to start putting the whole business behind us now. There's going to be no more talk about what could have been or should have been or who should have said what or why or when—What you've done, you've done. And that's that.

KAREN. *(Turns to him.)* What *I've* done?

CARDIN. *(Rises, moves R. Impatiently.)* What's been done to you.

KAREN. *(Follows him.)* You said it yesterday, too. What do you mean when you say "What you've done"? Tell me, darling. Tell me what you mean.

CARDIN. *(Turns to Karen. Shouting.)* Nothing. Nothing. I don't mean anything. Why do you think I do? *(Moves U. C. Then quietly.)* Karen, there are a lot of people in this world who have bad trouble. We happen to be three of those people. *(Turns to Karen.)* We could sit around the rest of our lives and live on that trouble, and we'd get to the place where we'd have nothing else because we wanted nothing else. That's fun for some people—but not for me. I wanted to be a doctor because I don't like sick people. *(Comes back to Karen, embraces her.)* I'm not going to be a sick man, and I'm not going to let you grow sick, either.

KAREN. I'm sorry. I'll be all right when we get out of here. *(Moves L. to below desk.)* I want a baby. I want to have a baby.

CARDIN. *(Laughs.)* We'll wait a year. We won't have enough money now.

KAREN. *(Turns to Cardin.)* I don't want to wait a year. You always said you wanted children right away. Why have you changed?

CARDIN. *(Slowly.)* We can't go on like this. Everything I say is made to mean something else. What are you doing to me? What's the matter with you?

KAREN. *(Quietly.)* Yes, every word has a new meaning. Child, love, lawyer, judge, friend, room, woman— *(Turns away L.)* There are not many safe words anymore. That we can't move away from. A new place, a new room, won't fix that for us. Sick, high-tragic people. That's what we'll be.

CARDIN. *(Crosses to Karen.)* No. No, we won't, darling. We must learn how to live and love again. We knew how to do it. It's only this bad time that has to be got over—We must go slow and take care, and it will pass quick—

KAREN. People don't set a date for things to go right or wrong. *(Moves away R.)* It won't work.

CARDIN. What won't work?

KAREN. The two of us together.

CARDIN. Stop talking like that. You'll believe it soon.

KAREN. Tell me. *(Turns to Cardin.)* Tell me what you want to know.

CARDIN. I don't know what you're talking about.

KAREN. Yes, you do. We've both known for a long time. Say it now, Joe. Ask it now.

CARDIN. I have nothing to ask. *(Neither speaks. He turns facing U. L.)*

KAREN. *(Holds his D.S. arm, leans her head on his shoulder.)* After a while, in the court, I stopped listening. After a while, it didn't seem to matter what anybody said. Then I began to watch your face. It was the only nice thing I could think of doing. You were ashamed. So was I. But you had trouble worse than that. You were sad at being ashamed. Ask it now, Joe.

CARDIN. I have nothing to ask. Nothing. *(Then, very quickly, turns to her.)* All right. It is—? Was it ever—?

KAREN. *(Quickly puts her hand over his mouth, stopping him.)* No. Martha and I have never touched each other. That's all right, darling. I'm not mad. I am glad you asked me.

CARDIN. My God, what's happened to me? *(Embraces her.)* I'm sorry, darling, I'm sorry. I didn't want to hurt you—I didn't ever believe— *(Crosses to C.)*

KAREN. No, of course you didn't, really. But after a while, you weren't sure. Maybe there was just a little truth—That's the way these things go. That's the way they are meant to go. You've been a good, loyal friend. *(Turns L.)* Don't be ashamed of what you felt. You're a fine man.

CARDIN. *(Crosses to Karen.)* I've asked, you've answered. That's all. Let's go ahead now and—

KAREN. You believe me?

CARDIN. *(With force.)* You know I believe you.

KAREN. Maybe you do. But I'd never know whether you did. And your saying it again won't do it. And it doesn't even matter anymore whether you do believe me. *(Moves away L.)* All that I know is that I'd be frightened you didn't. But that's the way it would be. We'd be hounded by it. You don't get over things by just saying you do. I don't believe you could touch my arm without my wondering why you didn't kiss me, and I don't think you could kiss me without my wondering if you really wanted to. And I'd hate myself for all that. And then I'd hate you, too. *(Turns to Cardin.)* I don't want ruin. I don't like it. *(Softly.)* Ah, Joe. You know all that.

CARDIN. *(Moves toward her.)* I don't. I don't.

KAREN. *(Softly.)* Ah, what happens between people, happens, and after a while it doesn't much matter how it started. But there it is. *(Turns U.S.)* I'm here. You're there. We're in a room we've been in so many times before. Nothing seems changed. My hands look just the same, my face is just the same, even my dress is old. I'm nothing too much: I'm like everybody else, the way I always was. I can have the things that other people have. I can have you, and children, and I can take care of them, and I can go to market, and read a book, and people will talk to me—Only I can't. I can't. And I don't know why. *(Turns L.)* Go home, darling.

CARDIN. *(Crosses to Karen, puts arms around her. With great force:)* We can't leave each other. We're not going to leave each other. You're tired. I'm tired. I didn't know what I was asking—

KAREN. Don't be sorry. *(Softly.)* You're such a nice man.

CARDIN. You say I helped you. Help me now. Help me. Karen—

KAREN. *(Turns to him.)* All right. Go away for a little while. Away from me and love and pity, and all the things that mess people up. Go away by yourself. And so will I. Please. Please do it that way. And after a while, I'll know and you'll know, and then we'll see—Please, Joe.

CARDIN. *(After a pause.)* There's nothing for me to know. A few weeks won't make any difference—

KAREN. Please.

CARDIN. I don't want to go.

KAREN. *(Turns L.)* Go now, darling.

CARDIN. What will you do?

KAREN. I'll wait. I'll be all right.

CARDIN. *(Kisses her hair.)* I'll be coming back soon. *(Exits U. C., leaving door open.)*

KAREN. *(A pause after he exits.)* I don't think so. *(She sits in D. L. chair quietly. After a moment Martha comes in with small tray and dust-cloth.)*

MARTHA. *(Goes to lamp on D. L. table, lights it.)* It gets dark so early now. *(Crosses to desk, puts down tray, empties ashtray into it.)* Cooking always makes me feel better. I found some purple scylla for the table. Remember! They were the first things we planted here. And I made a small cake. Know what? I found a bottle of wine. We'll have a good dinner. *(Crosses to below R. end of sofa, picks newspaper up from floor. No answer. She crosses back to above desk.)* Where's Joe?

KAREN. Gone.

MARTHA. *(Puts newspaper on desk.)* A patient? Will he be back in time for dinner?

KAREN. No.

MARTHA. *(Watching her.)* We'll wait dinner for him, then. Karen! What's the matter?

KAREN. *(In a dull tone.)* He won't be back.

MARTHA. *(Speaking slowly, carefully.)* You mean he won't be back any more tonight? *(Slowly crossing L. above desk.)*

KAREN. He won't be back at all.

MARTHA. *(Quickly, walks to R. of Karen.)* What happened? *(Karen shakes head.)* What happened, Karen?

KAREN. He thought we had been lovers.

MARTHA. *(Tensely.)* I don't believe you. I don't believe it. What kind of awful talk is that? I don't believe you. *I don't believe it.*

KAREN. All right, all right.

MARTHA. Didn't you tell him? For God's sake, didn't you tell him it wasn't true?

KAREN. Yes.

MARTHA. He didn't believe you?

KAREN. I guess he believed me.

MARTHA. *(Moves U.S. Angrily.)* Then what have you done? It's all wrong. It's crazy. I don't understand what you've done. You "guess" that he believed you. *(Comes back to R. of Karen.)* There's no guessing about it. Why didn't you—?

KAREN. I don't want ever to talk about it, Martha.

MARTHA. *(Sits in chair L. of desk.)* Oh God, I wanted that for you so much!

KAREN. Don't carry on. I don't feel well.

MARTHA. What's happened to us? What's really happened to us?

KAREN. I don't know. I think I'll make a cup of tea and go to bed now.

MARTHA. Whatever happened, go back to Joe. It's too much for you this way.

KAREN. *(Irritably.)* Stop talking about it. Let's pack and get out of here. Let's take the train in the morning.

MARTHA. The train to where?

KAREN. I don't know. Some place; any place.

MARTHA. A job? Money!

KAREN. In a big place we could get something to do.

MARTHA. They'd know about us. We've been in the headlines. We're very famous.

KAREN. A small town, then.

MARTHA. They'd know more about us, I guess.

KAREN. We'll find a place to go.

MARTHA. I don't think we will. Not really. I feel as if I couldn't move, and what would be the use? It seems to me I'll be sitting the rest of my life, wondering what happened. It's a bad night, tonight, but we might as well get used to it. They'll all be like this.

KAREN. *(Gets up, goes to stove. Hands in front of it, warming herself.)* But it isn't a new sin they tell us we've done. Other people aren't destroyed by it.

MARTHA. They are the people who believe in it, who want it, who've chosen it for themselves. That must be very different. We aren't like that. We don't love each other. We don't love each other. We've been close to each other, of course. I've loved you like a friend, the way thousands of women feel about other women.

KAREN. *(Turns her back to stove.)* I'm cold.

MARTHA. You were a dear friend who was loved, that's all. Certainly there's nothing wrong with that. It's perfectly natural that I should be fond of you. Why, we've known each other since we were seventeen and I always thought—

KAREN. *(As if she were tired.)* Why are you saying all this?

MARTHA. Because I love you.

KAREN. *(Sits on D. L. chair.)* Yes, of course. I love you, too.

MARTHA. But maybe I love you *that* way. The way they said I loved you. I don't know—Listen to me.

KAREN. What?

MARTHA. *(Kneels down next to Karen.) I have loved you the way they said.*

KAREN. *(Idly.)* Martha, we're both so tired. Please don't—

MARTHA. There's always been something wrong. Always—as long as I can remember. But I never knew it until all this happened.

KAREN. *(For first time looks up, horrified, turns to Martha.)* Stop that crazy talk—

MARTHA. You're afraid of hearing it; I'm more afraid than you.

KAREN. *(Turns away, hands over her ears.)* I won't listen to you.

MARTHA. You've got to know it. I can't keep it to myself any longer. I've got to tell you that I'm guilty.

KAREN. *(Deliberately.)* You are guilty of nothing.

MARTHA. I've been telling myself that since the night we heard the child say it. I lie in bed night after night praying that it isn't true. But I know about it now. It's there. I don't know how. I don't know why. But I did love you. I do love you. I resented your marriage; maybe because I wanted you; maybe I wanted you all these years; I couldn't call it by a name but maybe it's been there ever since I first knew you—

KAREN. *(Tensely, grips arms of chair.)* It's not the truth. Not a word of it. We never thought of each other that way.

MARTHA. *(Bitterly.)* No, of course *you* didn't. But who says I didn't? I never felt that way about anybody but you. I've never loved a man— *(Stops. Softly.)* I never knew why before. Maybe it's that.

KAREN. *(Carefully.)* You are tired and sick.

MARTHA. *(As though talking to herself.)* It's funny. It's all mixed up. There's something in you and you don't do anything about it because you don't know it's there. Suddenly a little girl gets bored and tells a lie—and there, that night, you see it for the first time, and you say it yourself, did she see it, did she sense it—?

KAREN. *(Turns to Martha. Desperately.)* What are you saying? You know it could have been any lie. She was looking for anything—

MARTHA. Yes, but why this one? She found the lie with the ounce of truth. I guess they always do. I've ruined your life and I've ruined my own. I swear I didn't know it, I swear I didn't mean it *(Rises, crosses U. L. in a wail.)* Oh, I feel so God-damned sick and dirty—I can't stand it anymore.

KAREN. All this isn't true. We don't have to remember it was ever said. Tomorrow we'll pick ourselves up and—

MARTHA. I don't want tomorrow. It's a bad word.

KAREN. *(Who is crying.)* Go and lie down, Martha. And in a few minutes, I'll make some tea and bring it to you. You'll feel better.

MARTHA. *(Looks around room, slowly, carefully. She is now very quiet. Moves, turns, looks at Karen.)* Don't bring me any tea. Thank you. Good night, darling. *(Martha exits L. Karen sits alone without moving. There is no sound in the house, until, a few moments after Martha's exit, a shot is heard. The sound of the shot should not be too loud or too strong, the act has not been sensational. For a few seconds after the noise has died out, Karen does not move. Then, suddenly, she springs from chair, and runs out L. Almost at same moment, footsteps are heard on staircase.)*

MRS. MORTAR. What was that? Where is it? *(Enters door C., frightened, aimlessly moving about.)* Karen! Martha! Where are you? I heard a shot. What was—? *(Stops as she sees Karen reappear from L. Walks toward her, still talking. Stops when she sees Karen's face.)* What—what is it? *(Karen moves her hands, shakes head slightly, passes Mrs. Mortar, goes toward window. Mrs. Mortar stares at her for a moment, rushes past her through door L. Left alone, Karen looks out window. Mrs. Mortar reenters crying, crosses to above chair L. of desk. After a moment.)* What shall we do? What shall we do?

KAREN. *(In a toneless voice.)* Nothing.

MRS. MORTAR. We've got to get a doctor—right away.

KAREN. *(Without turning.)* There isn't any use.

MRS. MORTAR. We've got to do something. Karen! Do something.

KAREN. There is nothing to do.

MRS. MORTAR. *(Crosses above desk to C.)* Oh, it's awful! Poor Martha. I don't know what we can do—You think she's dea—

KAREN. Yes.

MRS. MORTAR. Poor, poor Martha. *(Exits up C., starts upstairs.)* I can't realize it's true. Oh, how could she—she was so— *(Stops, comes back into the room.)* I don't know what— *(Looks up, still crying, surprised.)* I'm—I'm frightened. I'm frightened.

KAREN. Don't be frightened.

MRS. MORTAR. *(Sits in chair R. of desk.)* I can't help it. How can I help it? *(Gradually the sobs cease, and she sits, rocking herself.)* I'll never forgive myself for the last words I said to her. But I was good to her, Karen, and you know God will excuse me for that once. I always tried to do everything I could. *(Suddenly.)* Suicide's a sin. Karen, we can't sit here. *(No answer. Timidly.)* Shouldn't we call somebody to—?

KAREN. *(Slowly turns, crosses to below sofa.)* In a little while.

MRS. MORTAR. She shouldn't have done it, she shouldn't have done it. It was because of all this awful business. She would have got a job and started all over again—she was just worried and sick and—

KAREN. That isn't the reason she did it.

MRS. MORTAR. What—Why?

KAREN. *(Wearily, sits R. end of sofa.)* What difference does it make now?

MRS. MORTAR. *(Reproachfully.)* You're not crying...

KAREN. No.

MRS. MORTAR. *(Rises, moves to in front of desk.)* Oh, I wish I could have done something. But I haven't anything, you know.

KAREN. She was good to you; she was good to me.

MRS. MORTAR. Oh, I know she was, Karen, and I was good to her, too. I did everything I could. I—I haven't any place to go.

KAREN. I'll help you.

MRS. MORTAR. *(After a few seconds of silence, she moves U. C.)* We must do something. I'm afraid. It seems so queer—in the next room. *(Shivers.)*

KAREN. Don't be afraid.

MRS. MORTAR. It's different for you. You're young. *(The sound of doorbell ringing. Mrs. Mortar jumps. Karen doesn't move. Nervously.)* Who is it? *(Bell rings again.)* Shall I answer it? I think we'd better. *(Exits R. down hall. Her voice is heard from offstage.)* Oh! Oh! You can't come in here... Go away...go away... What are you doing here? *(Comes back into room.)* It's that woman. It's that Mrs. Tilford. I told her to go away. She says she's been trying to get in all day. *(Mrs. Tilford appears in doorway. Mrs. Mortar turns to her.)* We've had trouble here.

MRS. TILFORD. Let me come in, please.

MRS. MORTAR. *(Crosses to her, tries to block her way.)* I say you can't come in. You...

MRS. TILFORD. *(Crosses down to L. of sofa.)* Move away, please. Karen, I've something to say to you. You must hear me. *(Mrs. Mortar goes U. L., leans against bookcase, facing upstage.)*

KAREN. Why have you come here?

MRS. TILFORD. I had to come. I've been outside all day... I've been at the door... I've been phoning you... I tried to speak to Joe, but he won't talk to me. I've been waiting for you to come out. Then I thought I heard a shot, or something, but...

KAREN. Get out of here.

MRS. MORTAR. *(Turns to Mrs. Tilford.)* You bad, bad woman.

You have no right in this house. You don't know what you've done. MRS. TILFORD. Please be still. *(Mrs. Mortar, her face in her hands, exits L. down hall.)* Karen, you must let me speak. I know it wasn't true. I found out it wasn't true. Mrs. Wells came to me today with…

KAREN. *(Stares at her, shudders.)* You know it wasn't true, do you? I don't care what you know. If that's what you had to say, you've said it. Go away.

MRS. TILFORD. *(Moves to below L. end of sofa.)* I've got to tell you.

KAREN. I don't want to hear you.

MRS. TILFORD. Mrs. Wells found a bracelet in Rosalie's room. The bracelet had been hidden for several months. She found out that Rosalie had taken the bracelet from another girl, and that Mary— *(Closes her eyes.)* that Mary knew that and used it to force Rosalie into saying that she had seen you and Miss Dobie together. I—I've talked to Mary. I found out.

KAREN. *(In a loud voice.)* Go away, Mrs. Tilford. Get out of here.

MRS. TILFORD. I have only a little more to say. I've talked to Judge Potter. He has made all arrangements. There will be a public apology and an explanation. The damage suit will be paid to you in full and—and any more that you will be kind enough to take from me. He's waiting to talk to you. We will do whatever you say.

KAREN. Martha is dead. *(Mrs. Tilford gasps, shakes head, very slowly, sits L. end of sofa, covers face. Karen watches her.)* So last night you found out you had done wrong to us. And now you have to right that wrong or you can't rest your head again. Well, don't rest it. I won't be your confessor. Take your conscience some place else, get somebody else to help you be a "good" woman again. *(Smiles.)* You told us that night you had to do what you did. Now you have to do this. A public apology and money paid and you can sleep and eat again. You and all those who always know how right they are. What's somebody else's life to you? A way to show your own righteousness. And if you happen to be wrong, *(Shrugs.)* then you can always put it right some other day. *(Quietly.)* I have a dead friend. Get out of here and be noble on the street.

MRS. TILFORD. *(Slowly shakes head.)* There is no relief for me, and there never will be again. I didn't come here for that. I swear to God I did not. But what I am or why I came doesn't make any difference. Doesn't matter. All that matters is you and—You now. Help me, Karen.

KAREN. *(Smiles.)* Help you?

MRS. TILFORD. Let me do whatever I can do. Take whatever I can give. It won't bring me peace, and you don't think it will. I'm too old to recover, too narrow to forgive myself.

KAREN. *(After a pause.)* Yes. I believe you. You will have a hard time ahead.

MRS. TILFORD. I will.

KAREN. Mary?

MRS. TILFORD. I don't know. I don't know what to do. People say—I've read—but I can't believe or understand it. I—I'll just—I don't know.

KAREN. She's yours. *(Smiles.)* Blood of your blood, the result of you. Yes, it will be hard for a woman like you. She's harmed us both, but she did you the most harm. *(Softly.)* I guess I'm even sorry.

MRS. TILFORD. You will try for yourself?

KAREN. *(Wearily.)* Yes, I will.

MRS. TILFORD. Come away now. You can't stay with—

KAREN. No, I don't want to go.

MRS. TILFORD. You'll be all right?

KAREN. *(Slowly rises, crosses to above chair U. L. of D. R. table. Looks out window.)* Yes. Goodbye, now. I don't want to see you again.

MRS. TILFORD. *(Slowly rises, crosses U. C. Turns to Karen.)* But you'll let me help you? You'll let me try?

KAREN. If it will make you feel better.

MRS. TILFORD. Yes, yes, yes. Will you write to me some time?

KAREN. *(Not turning from window.)* If I ever have anything to say.

MRS. TILFORD. You will have something to say. Goodbye, my dear child.

KAREN. Goodbye. *(Mrs. Tilford slowly exits U.S. as curtain falls.)*

CURTAIN

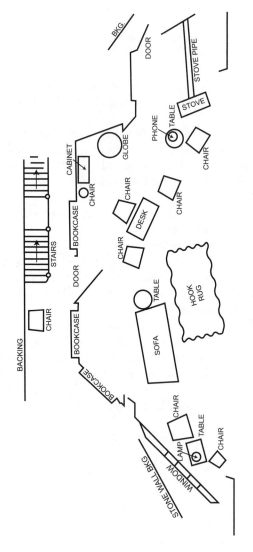

SCENE DESIGN — ACTS I and III

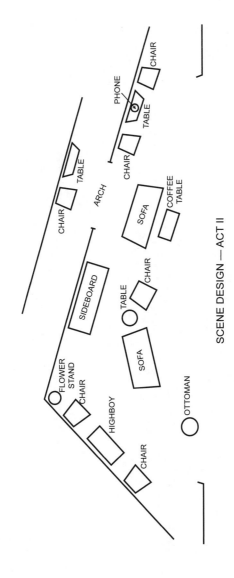

SCENE DESIGN — ACT II

NOTES
(Use this space to make notes for your production)

NOTES

(Use this space to make notes for your production)

NOTES
(Use this space to make notes for your production)

NOTES

(Use this space to make notes for your production)

NOTES
(Use this space to make notes for your production)